A Gentlemen's Guide to Style and Self-Defense in the Old American West

By James M. Volo, PhD

A Man of the West, future president Teddy Roosevelt (1893)

The Traditional American History Series
No. 14

To my nephews and their children
So they might know the America that I have known.

The Traditional American History Series
Affordable books dedicated to the History of American Exceptionalism
By James M. Volo, PhD

The God of Democracy,
Religion in Revolutionary America, No. 1

Stand Alarmed,
Militia in America, 1608-1783, No. 2

From Whence the Silver,
The Role of Money in Colonial America, No. 3

They Came to Sing,
Music in the Colonies, 1607-1787, No. 4

Slow But Deadly
The Dive-bombers of World War II, No. 5

To Bend the Bow of Ulysses
Wade Hampton's Southern Cavalry, No. 6

Soldiers of the Press
Civil War Journalism, 1861-1865, No. 7

Custer's Civil War Cavalry
Forged by Fire, United By Will, No. 8

And other titles.

This book **DOES NOT** promote, encourage, or condone ethnic, racial, religious or sectional animosity or stereotyping. It **DOES** uphold traditional values of patriotism, personal ethics, honor, and devotion to the production and representation of authentic American history.

EZ-Read format

A Gentlemen's Guide to Style and Self-Defense in the Old American West

By James M. Volo, PhD

Legendary actor John Wayne as he first appeared *Stagecoach* (1939).

Stagecoach was the first of many Westerns that John Ford shot in black and white using Monument Valley in the American southwest as a location and background. Many of Ford's later films would be in color. No director of the sound era made as many great films more quickly than Ford did when he followed *Stagecoach* with three nominations and two Oscars for directing before the end of World War II. The film has a fair claim to be the most influential Western ever made. The 1939 version of *Stagecoach* was deemed culturally and historically significant by the Library of Congress and selected for preservation in its National Film Registry.

Seen today, *Stagecoach* may not seem very original. That's because it influenced countless later Western movies and remakes in which a mixed bag of characters are thrown together by chance and forced to survive an ordeal. The genre, known as an "ensemble movie" at times plays like an anthology of timeless clichés, yet the personal interaction of real people in the Old West often brought together such groups with diverse backgrounds and diametrically opposed goals.

Preface for the Discriminating Gentleman

The appellation of Gentleman should never be affixed to a man's circumstances, but rather to his behavior in them.

— Sir Richard Steele, 1710

The Old West has had a powerful impact on the concept of gentlemanly masculinity among Americans. To behave like a gentleman may mean little or much. To spend large sums of money like a gentleman may be of no great praise, but to conduct ones self like a gentleman implies a high standard even for those without financial means. For almost two centuries, the frontiersman has been a standard of rugged individualism and stoic bravery for the American male. Provider, protector, counselor, and knight errant to the weak or helpless, men on the frontier stood apart. Newspapers, Dime Novels, and Wild West Shows helped to form the popular view of Old West masculinity in the later 19th century. Novels and short stories served this purpose in the first half of the 20th century, but it was films and TV that cemented the image of the Old west that most post WWII Baby Boomers have today.

The study of film and other media representations has been a particularly energetic field for masculinity research. However, western films are not so much about the West as they are about the Westerner. He stands alone, heroic, powerful, and seeking justice and order. The Westerner is the "last gentleman" and Westerns are "probably the last art form in which the concept of honor retains its strength." Directors and screenwriters, ultimately having overcome the simplistic shoot-em-up, used the genre to explore the pressing subjects of their day like racism, nationalism, capitalism, family, and honor – issues more deeply meshed with the concept of manliness than simply wearing a gun belt and Stetson hat.[1]

Fear not, Old West purists! For those traditionalists amongst you, these pages are filled with authentic designs, facts, weapons, and tales from the mid 1800s to the turn of the century and slightly beyond. Here are some of the roots of the most popular holsters, fashions, weapons, cartridges, and myths preferred by collectors and re-enactors. So-called Cowboy Action enthusiasts, NRA members, and armchair generals will find sections of this work devoted to their hobbies, and while stodgy academics might cringe, Old West historians will have their obsessions somewhat mollified. Nonetheless, the current author grew up in the days of Shoot'em-up Saturdays at the movies, prime time TV Westerns, and those wondrous sights and sounds of Cowboy gunfights with cap guns on a hillside and Indian encounters on the pavement during a childhood when neither activity was considered politically incorrect. Few other authors in this genre have a résumé that includes formal training in science, weapons, and horsemanship; nor have they actually been a horse wrangler, ridden in a troop of cavalry, and reenacted a mounted charge with dozens of others, Hollywood cameras running, revolvers or swords in hand. Nonetheless, there comes a time when we are all "too old and too fat to jump rail fences with horses" (*True Grit*) and must retire to our easy chairs to write. What follows is a serious (if a bit nostalgic) effort at history by a critically noted author and widely published historian with the proper credentials and practical experience to attempt to carry it off. Cling to your Bibles and to your guns, partner! Dudes need not apply.

Introduction: Go West, Young Man.

My heroes have always been cowboys.

– Song by Waylon Jennings, 1976

The Oxford Dictionary of Quotations says that the newspaper editor Horace Greeley coined the phrase "Go West, young man. Go West!" in his 1850 book *Hints Toward Reform*, and that subsequently John B. L. Soule used it in an 1851 editorial in the *Terre Haute Indiana Express*. *Bartlett's Quotations*, however, says that the Soule article inspired Greeley to use the quotation in an 1865 editorial in the *New York Tribune*. The exact words appear in none of these sources thereby fueling some "chicken vs. egg" controversy. Even earlier references are cited in a recent biography of Greeley: "If any young man is about to commence the world, we say to him, publicly and privately, 'Go to the West'" (from the 25 August 1838, issue of the *New Yorker*). "Go West, young man" may well have been a paraphrase of this earlier sentiment. Without regard to the source, in the latter half of the 19th century the national focus was clearly turned to the West.[2]

It is somewhat ironic that the major engineering accomplishment of the first half of the 19th century—having taken place in the East—should have been pivotal to the opening of the Trans-Mississippi West. Federal outlays in the early 19th century included support for a man-made waterway across central New York State from the Hudson River to Lake Erie. In 1825, the opening of the Erie Canal formed a convenient transportation link between the cities of the Northeast, the headwaters of the Ohio River, and via the Great Lakes to all the Midwest as far away as the Indian lands in Wisconsin and Minnesota. When English author Charles Dickens came to tour America in 1842, he considered his time in St. Louis as a visit to the West, but he did note the existence of "a very far west" some "little way" beyond the city.[3]

Nonetheless, travel to the territories beyond the Mississippi River remained difficult and dangerous, but Westward expansion along the growing system of canals and the successful navigation of the Western rivers by steamboats benefited the connections with both the states of the Midwest and the Western territories of the Great Plains and Rocky Mountains. A British pamphlet from 1820 erroneously noted, "Two hundred miles west of the Mississippi River … an extensive desert commences, which extends to the Pacific Ocean." The editors in London reported the growing city of St. Louis to be on the outermost edge of feasible civilized development. Little did they know![4]

Admittedly, the Mexican War of 1846, the Gold Rush of 1849, and the aftermath of the Civil War (1861-1865) accelerated the movement west beyond most period assumptions. The development of steam locomotion and the completion of the transcontinental telegraph and railroad further opened the West. Historians noted in 1894 that in its infancy, the United States had relied on its foreign trade and maritime connections with Europe almost as a toddler clings to a "security blanket." They suggested that the nation now stood with its back to the waterways and exalted the ribbons of steel to the West. In a more mobile 19th-century world, emigration and resettlement were becoming commonplace. In a wildly expanding nation, the call of cheap land, personal freedom, or stirring adventure caused many young men and women to leave the confines of their parental homes and stretch the bonds of family support.[5]

Purpose: Are You a Teddy Roosevelt or a John Wayne?

The purpose of this book is to provide insight into the Old American West, its qualities, its symbols, and its people—both real persons and those that populate our myths and traditions. In two men popular with Western aficionados, John Wayne and Theodore Roosevelt, fiction and fact make a fortuitous nexus for the purposes of this discussion.

As the fictional character J.B. Books, an aging gunfighter in the movie *The Shootist* (1976), actor John Wayne describes a masculine ethos that would probably be acceptable to most real men living in the Old West in the previous century: "I won't be wronged. I won't be insulted. I won't be laid a-hand on. I don't do these things to other people, and I require the same from them." Seemingly no statement better encapsulates the popular concept of Western masculinity. The character Books may not consider himself a hero, but he appears to consider his actions necessary and just, given the circumstances of the time and place.[6]

Yet Wayne's role in an earlier film, *The Man Who Shot Liberty Valance* (1962) with James Stewart (portraying Ransom Stoddard, a non-violent man made an accidental hero in a gunfight by circumstance) was probably a more appropriate tribute to the passing of the Old West. "This is the West, sir. When a legend becomes fact, print the legend." The point made by director John Ford in the film is that we are often more comfortable with treasured legends than with hard truths. That quote from the latter film is a great one, especially when it comes to taking a closer look at historical memory and its impact on American attitudes toward Old West style masculinity.[7]

Frequently described as being about a dying gunman's attempt to face death with dignity in the not so wild west of 1901, *The Shootist* is indeed about the last days of an aging gunman (John Bernard Books played by John Wayne) and his desire for an end with dignity. Set just as word of the death of Queen Victoria has been received (January), the movie is about the end of ages and the passing of icons on many levels. Horses are being replaced by automobiles, kerosene lamps by electricity, and stagecoaches by streetcars. Later in 1901 (September), President William McKinley would die at the hand of an assassin, and Theodore Roosevelt would become President. Roosevelt had become famous during the Spanish-American War and later as Vice-President for his own quotation: "Speak softly and carry a Big Stick." Roosevelt thereafter used military muscle several times throughout his two terms as President with a more subtle touch to complement his diplomatic Big Stick policies.

As word spreads that the famous gunman Books has incurable cancer, an assortment of human vultures gathers to feast on the corpse among them a coldhearted gambler, an unrepentant rustler, a hypocritical clergyman, a scheming undertaker, a jaded lover, a "yellow press" journalist, even a sycophantic teenager. Set against this ensemble of clichés is a good, warmhearted, and sympathetic woman played by Lauren Bacall. Both Bacall and Wayne knew at the time of the filming that the legendary western actor might soon die of cancer and that in all likelihood this would be his last screen portrayal—a brilliant career-finishing movie. The actor had had a smoker's lung removed twelve years earlier and was now struggling with the stomach cancer that would eventually lead to his death. He died three years after the film's release. Shortly before his death at just 62 years of age, the US Congress approved a congressional gold medal for Wayne—the highest governmental honor available to ordinary persons. It is awarded to those who have performed an achievement that has an impact on American history and culture. Certainly this is part of his legacy.[8]

Those readers who have an affinity for John Wayne because they grew up with him on the silver screen or TV, should also appreciate Teddy Roosevelt. As a leader of the Republican Party at the turn of the century, Theodore Roosevelt became a driving force for the Progressive Era in the United States in the early 20th century. Roosevelt successfully overcame the health problems of his childhood by embracing a strenuous and vigorous lifestyle. He integrated his exuberant personality, vast range of interests, and world-famous achievements into a "cowboy" persona defined by a robust and authentic masculinity. Neither unusually tall nor lanky in a John Wayne Western sense, TR escaped to the wilderness of the American West operating a cattle ranch in the Dakotas for a time, before returning East to run unsuccessfully for Mayor of New York City in 1886. At one point he had established a herd of 1600 steers. On the banks of the Little Missouri, Roosevelt learned to ride western style, rope cattle, and hunt. He generally earned the respect of authentic cowboys, but failed to deal with the economic downturn that ultimately made his ranch a failure. As a deputy sheriff, Roosevelt once pursued three outlaws who had stolen his riverboat and escaped north up the Little Missouri. He captured them, but decided against a vigilante hanging. Instead, he assumed guard over them for forty hours without sleep, while reading Leo Tolstoy to keep himself awake, and conveyed them to trial.

Prior to his service in the Spanish–American War, Roosevelt had already received military training with the New York National Guard. Commissioned on 1 August 1882 as a 2nd Lieutenant with B Company, 8th Regiment, he was promoted to Captain and company commander a year later, and he remained in command until he resigned his commission in 1886. When the United States and Spain declared war against each other in late April 1898, Roosevelt resigned from his civilian leadership job as Assistant Secretary of the Navy and formed the Rough Riders (First US Volunteer Cavalry Regiment) along with Army Colonel Leonard Wood. Under Roosevelt's leadership, the Rough Riders became famous for the charge up Kettle Hill (Cuba) on 1 July 1898, while supporting the regulars.

Returning from the Army, he won the race for Governor of New York. Although he had anticipated a second term as governor, he was chosen to run as Vice-President on the GOP ticket with William McKinley in 1900. The office of Vice President was a powerless sinecure, and seemingly did not suit Roosevelt's aggressive temperament. Following the assassination of President McKinley in September 1901, however, Roosevelt succeeded to the office, becoming the youngest (age 42) US President in history. In 1905, Roosevelt, an admirer of various western figures, named Captain Bill McDonald of the Texas Rangers as his personal bodyguard and entertained many legendary westerners at the White House. After leaving office at the end of a second term, Roosevelt went on safari in Africa and toured Europe. He then led a two-year expedition in the Amazon Basin, nearly dying of a tropical disease. He was a noted hunter of big game, but refused to shoot a black bear tied to a tree (the source of the famous Teddy Bear).

Roosevelt normally enjoyed very close relationships with the press, which he used to keep in daily contact with his middle-class base. While out of office, he made a living as a writer and magazine editor. His most ambitious book was the four-volume narrative *The Winning of the West* (written 1889-1896), which focused on the American frontier in the 18th and early 19th centuries. Among his other works were books on the vigorous life of the West: *The Strenuous Life* (1900), *Hunting the Grisly* (1904), *The Wilderness Hunter* (1893), and *Ranch Life and the Hunting Trail* (1888), and many others. Roosevelt said that the American character – indeed a new "Americanism" had emerged from the heroic wilderness hunters and Indian fighters, acting on the frontier with little government help.

Roosevelt was the exemplar of American masculinity in his time. Historians credit Roosevelt for changing the nation's political system by permanently placing the presidency at center stage and making character as important as other issues. His friend, historian Henry Adams, proclaimed: "Roosevelt, more than any other man ... showed the singular primitive quality that belongs to ultimate matter—the quality that medieval theology assigned to God—he was pure action."[9]

Roosevelt left the presidential office in 1909, and although he attempted to run again he was not returned to office. In a speech given in Paris in 1910 (commonly known as *The Man in the Arena*), Teddy Roosevelt noted:

> It is not the critic who counts; not the man who points out how the strong man stumbles, or where the doer of deeds could have done them better. The credit belongs to the man who is actually in the arena, whose face is marred by dust and sweat and blood; who strives valiantly; who errs, who comes short again and again, because there is no effort without error and shortcoming; but who does actually strive to do the deeds; who knows great enthusiasms, the great devotions; who spends himself in a worthy cause; who at the best knows in the end the triumph of high achievement, and who at the worst, if he fails, at least fails while daring greatly, so that his place shall never be with those cold and timid souls who neither know victory nor defeat.[10]

The Old West period often includes a number of historic signposts for American history: the Texan War of Independence (1835-1836), the American-Mexican War (1846-1848), the Gold Rush (1849), the Civil War (1861-1865), the Transcontinental Telegraph (1861) and Railroad (1869), the Centennial Year (1876), the Indian Wars of the second half of the 19th century, and the early part of the 20th century up to 1912, when the last contiguous mainland states of Arizona and New Mexico entered the Union. Roosevelt was a small boy during the Civil War and had relations fighting on both sides. It was said that he played soldier, pretending to be wounded but fighting on nonetheless. Yet he lived through much of the period of the Old West and was part of it.

John Wayne was a toddler when TR left office, but the period of Wayne's acting career between *Stagecoach* (1939) and *The Shootist* (1976) was also one of remarkable importance to the development of an exceptional American character, and character is that which the history of the Old West has left as an inheritance. Tested by the crises of Pearl Harbor (1941), WWII, Korea, the Cold War, and Vietnam, and the fall of Saigon (1975), America entered its bicentennial year with a résumé of victories and calamities, but the ethical and patriotic core of its population remained solid. These were aided, as pointed out by President Ronald Reagan, by a healthy sense of Americanism as infused into the popular culture by films and TV.

Note: There are few who would question Wayne's lasting contribution to the American character and culture. Yet as recently as 2016 the California legislature has denied Wayne several posthumous awards in memoriam largely because he professed a conservative Democratic politics at the time of his death. In almost the same breath, the Hollywood elite has announced an outrageous film project—a so-called comedy—that will poke fun at Republican Ronald Reagan and his difficulties late in his Presidency with the onset of Alzheimer's disease. How far we have come! How sad and troubling!

Populating the West

Advice author J. Clinton Ransom, writing from the perspective of the late 1880s, believed that a gentleman's natural attributes fitted him for his profession and for his place in society. He wrote, "We do not believe that all men, or any considerable number of men, could enter upon ... totally different lines of action and succeed in all." A man who followed his vocation for a lifetime "with utter faithfulness" and "mastered the duties around him" could expect no surprises as he arrived at eminence and social respectability. A man who lost his place at business, or failed in his profession also lost part of his masculine identity. The author was speaking to those he considered gentlemen in his audience. It is unlikely that Ransom was considering cowboys, lawmen, gamblers and desperados when he wrote his thesis, but much of what he said was still significant. In the 19th century, the period of a gentleman's life known today as the *Mid-life Crisis* was often resolved with a migration to the West rather than with a new sports car or a trophy wife. Many of those who moved west attempted to reinvent themselves or just lose their former selves amongst the great expanse of new territories.[11]

In his frontier thesis of 1893, eminent historian Frederick Jackson Turner noted, "American social development has been continually beginning over again on the frontier. This perennial rebirth, this fluidity of American life, this expansion westward with its new opportunities, its continuous touch with the simplicity of primitive society, furnishes the forces dominating American character. ... The frontier is the line of most rapid and effective Americanization. ... It appears then that the universal disposition of Americans [is] to emigrate to the western wilderness, in order to enlarge their dominion over inanimate nature."[12]

Nowhere was a man's character more important or more sorely tested, than on the emigrant trails to the West. Good judgment, integrity of purpose, and practical application thereof were indispensable to the harmony of the wagon train and the successful completion of the journey. Captain Randolph B. Marcy, a popular advisor to prairie travelers, wrote in 1859, "On long and arduous expeditions men are apt to become irritable and ill-natured, and oftentimes fancy they have more labor imposed upon them then their comrades. ... That man who exercises the greatest forbearance under such circumstances, who is cheerful, slow to take up quarrels, and endeavors to reconcile difficulties among his companions, is deserving of all praise, and will, no doubt, contribute largely to the success and comfort of an expedition."[13]

It was said that the Old West occupied the prime location between coastal California and the middle of nowhere. Into this vast area was funneled a diverse mix of professions, nationalities, races, political views, and religions that could seemingly enter without rubbing someone else the wrong way. Nonetheless, the West often reflected the biases that divided the rest of the nation, and it would be a fiction to claim that the region was not filled with bigotry, prejudice, racism, and xenophobia. The polarization of persons was particularly extreme among those who held strong opinions regarding slavery and states' rights.

This 1884 photo shows TR standing in full Wild West regalia with his horse in the Badlands of Dakota Territory. Roosevelt originally came to North Dakota in hopes of killing a buffalo. The former president stayed on after becoming enamored with the rugged, beautiful territory of the badlands. His time there opened his eyes to the plight of the bison and other animals that were being hunted to near extinction. When he returned to New York to pursue a dual career as writer and public servant, Roosevelt began to lobby for conservation.

1. A Heritage of Violence

Unfortunately, restraint and bipartisanship were conspicuously absent during the Antebellum Period. Antagonists on all sides assailed their opponents with arguments taken from the law, the Bible, literature, pamphlets, election speeches, and a highly partisan press. When unprepared to rebut these arguments on an equal footing, the opponents often resorted to ridiculous remarks, unsupported allegations, fisticuffs, or firearms. Many encounters would have been comical had the underlying issues not been so serious. When Senator Charles Sumner, a man of "wicked tongue" and "intemperate language" with regard to slavery, was beaten with a cane by Congressman Preston Brooks in the Senate (1856), the blows were struck not only in the halls of Congress, but in the barbershops, parlors, and taverns of every small town and city.

At mid-century the West was further East than most persons would surmise. Only days after the Kansas-Nebraska Act was passed in 1854, pro-slavery and anti-slavery supporters rushed in to settle the area, both sides hoping to affect the outcome of the first election. Because the act stated that the future status of slavery in the two territories was to be decided by popular vote, the opposing sides competed to win the region for their political beliefs. Nebraska was considered to be too far north to be brought into the southern fold, but Kansas was on a knife's edge between free and slave. After the invasion of the Kansas polls by the proslavery forces at the election of 1855, the free-state settlers began to organize to defend their rights. In Lawrence two companies, of about fifty members each, were formed and an agent was dispatched to Boston to secure arms.

The name "Beecher's Bibles" was used during this period in reference to the technologically advanced Sharps breech-loading carbines and rifles purchased by anti-slavery organizations through the auspices of Henry Ward Beecher, a noted abolitionist minister who sponsored the New England Emigrant Aid Society. The Society disguised shipments of arms intended for Kansas in crates marked "Tools" and in boxes identified as "machinery" and even in "German immigrant trunks." The arms purchased were, on at least one occasion, shipped in wooden crates marked "books," though there is no verifiable evidence that any firearms were shipped in boxes marked "Bibles." On 8 February 1856, an article in the *New York Tribune* noted:

> He [Beecher] believed that the Sharps Rifle was a truly moral agency, and that there was more moral power in one of those instruments, so far as the slaveholders of Kansas were concerned, than in a hundred Bibles. You might just as well ... read the Bible to Buffaloes as to those [pro-slavery] fellows who follow [David Rice] Atchison and [Benjamin] Stringfellow; but they have a supreme respect for the logic that is embodied in a Sharp's rifle.

During the border trouble of 1856, the free-state groups were continually in the field. They participated in the attack on the proslavery forces at New Georgia and at Franklin, and they took part in the capture of Fort Saunders and Fort Titus. On the return journey to Lawrence, they were captured by federal troops, marched to Lecompton, and imprisoned, some being confined for several months as an illegally constituted militia. After their release they continued their organization. During the 1856 conflict in Kansas, John Brown commanded forces at the town of Osawatomie when it came under attack by 200-400 border ruffians. With 40 or so men, Brown tried to defend the town against the proslavery partisans, causing heavy casualties before being forced to withdraw. This was one event in a series of clashes between abolitionists and pro-slavery Missourians. Brown's followers then killed five slavery supporters at Pottawatomie. These same abolitionists endorsed Brown's attempt to foment an armed slave rebellion in Virginia by attacking Harper's Ferry in 1858.

Among the "sovereign squats" were this group of Kansas gentlemen who had formed themselves into a local company of free-state militia. Most of the men were of short stature, hence the name. (c. 1855)[14]

Not to be outdone, Southerners fought just as hard to make Kansas a slave state. With slaveowner-friendly Missouri right next door, numerous proslavery settlers flooded across the border, many establishing Town Association Companies and forming some of the earliest cities, such as Leavenworth and Atchison. A number of "Blue Lodges," proslavery organizations, were formed in the South to assist in promoting the interests of the slave power. These societies were known by different names, such as the "Friends Society," the "Social Band," the "Dark Lantern Society," and the "Sons of the South." The order was thought to be a branch of the infamous Knights of the Golden Circle, the common object being the same—the extension of slavery. Another group called the Law and Order League, also known as the Army of Law and Order was formed ostensibly for the purpose of promoting peace, prosperity and good government among the people of Kansas. But, such was not the case. It was an armed force, the strength of which has been variously estimated at from 500 to 1000 men, whose policy was banishment or extermination of all free-state men in the territory.

The battles between the opposing parties continued until a referendum was finally authorized by the English Bill of 1858, which dashed all pro-slavery hopes of Kansas Territory becoming part of the slaveowning South. However, continued struggles would delay the admission of Kansas as a free state until January 1861. Thereafter, Kansas was justly regarded as a mere outpost in the larger war now being waged between the antagonistic civilizations of the North and the South.

When President Lincoln called for troops in May 1861, the free-state militias responded immediately. After filling their ranks, they proceeded to Fort Leavenworth, where they were mustered into the First Regiment of Kansas Volunteer Infantry. Within two months the First Regiment engaged in battle at Wilson creek, one of the most important battles in the West. It is doubtful whether any similar group had a sterner record of service in the Civil War. The editor of the *Kansas Tribune*, gave some interesting particulars concerning the regiment's remarkable record in the Civil War, asserting that the entire enrollment of the company contained 390 names since its first organization and the aggregate on their discharge was only eighty-nine. There were fifty-two promotions mostly from the original company, three to the rank of colonel. After the war the need for local militia companies ceased, and the ranks of the original regiment were too depleted, perhaps, to allow a continuation of the organization. At any rate, no account of their postwar meetings is to be found.[15]

The conflicts in Kansas have been well portrayed in a number of classic Western films, especially in *Dark Command* (1940), *The Outlaw Josey Wales* (1976), and *Ride With the Devil* (1999). Although the name "Red Legs" is commonly conflated with the term "jayhawkers" to describe Kansas guerilla units that fought for the Free-State side during the Bleeding Kansas era or the Union side in the Civil War, Red Legs originally referred to a specific paramilitary outfit that organized in Kansas at the height of the Civil War.

The Red Legs were a somewhat secretive organization of about 50 to 100 ardent abolitionists who were hand selected for harsh duties along the border. They commonly dressed in red leggings, plumed hats, long Federal-style tunic coats, and were armed with a myriad of pistols about their waists. Membership in the group was fluid and some of the men went on to serve in the 7th Kansas Cavalry or other regular army commands and state militias. They are associated with a lesser-known group that called themselves the "buckskin scouts," who served as an auxiliary arm to regular troops, such as the 6th Kansas Cavalry on punitive expeditions into Missouri. The Red Legs faded from the scene afterwards as guerilla war diminished along the border.

This stunning illustration captures the confusion and panic in a town hit by one of Quantrill's lightning fast raids. The illustration from *Harpers Illustrated* (September 27, 1862) is by Thomas Nast, one of the most famous artists of the 1800s. It captures many of the deprivations and atrocities attributed to the guerrillas.

When William Quantrill and his band of Southern bushwhackers attacked Lawrence, Kansas, on 16 August 1863, they cited the deeds of the Red Legs as among the motives for their attack on the town. One of the first targets of the bushwhackers was the headquarters of the Red Legs, the Johnson House Hotel. The Missouri-Kansas border area was so thoroughly devastated that it became known thereafter as the "Burnt District." Quantrill and his men thereafter rode south to Texas, where they lodged among the Confederate forces. While in Texas, Quantrill and his 400 men quarreled. His once-large band broke up into several smaller guerrilla companies. Many of Quantrill's men went on to become notorious western outlaws after the war.

Quantrill's actions remain controversial to this day. Some historians view him as an opportunistic, bloodthirsty outlaw. James M. McPherson, one of America's most prominent experts on the Civil War today, calls him a pathological killer who murdered and burned out Missouri Unionists. It is safe to say that the violence of the Civil War led to much of the seemingly indiscriminate violence seen in the Old West. Some of Quantrill's celebrity rubbed off on those among the ex-Raiders – John Jarrett, George and Oliver Shepard, Jesse and Frank James, and Cole Younger who went on after the war to apply Quantrill's hit-and-run tactics to bank and train robbery.

After the war, the James brothers had continued to associate with their old guerrilla comrades, who remained together under the leadership of Archie Clement. It was likely Clement who, amid the tumult of Reconstruction in Missouri, turned the guerrillas into outlaws. At various times, the so-called James Gang included the Younger brothers (Cole, Jim, John, and Bob), the two James brothers, John Jarrett (married to Cole's sister Josie), Bud and Donny Pence, Frank Gregg, Bill and James Wilkerson, Joab Perry, Ben Cooper, Red Mankus, Allen Parmer (who later married Susan James, Frank and Jesse's sister), Arthur McCoy, George Shepard, Oliver Shepard, William McDaniel, Tom McDaniel, Clell Miller, Charlie Pitts, and Bill Chadwell (alias Bill Stiles). On the other side of the ledger of Old West gunmen and desperados were the legendary "Wild Bill" Hickok, then still just a teenager, William "Buffalo Bill" Cody, and fellow Pony Express rider William S. Tough among the few individuals known to have served with the Red Legs.[16]

Native Americans

For many persons the antebellum frontier began at Fort Leavenworth, Kansas. Early in the century it was a largely vacant plain full of Indians, whose little shaggy ponies were tied by dozens among the houses and along the fences. Tribal members among the Sacs and Foxes, with shaved heads and painted faces, Shawnees and Delawares, fluttering in calico frocks and turbans, Wyandottes dressed in part like white men, and a few "wretched" Kansas tribesmen wrapped in old blankets strolled about the streets or lounged in and about the shops and houses. Yet these were Native Americans infected, some would say contaminated beyond redemption, by white European contact. These were not the great warrior nations of the Plains, nor were they the equals in warfare of the tribes of the Eastern Woodlands like the Iroquois, Huron, or Abenaki of an earlier century.[17]

From time to time, there were as many as 35 discrete tribes, groups, and subgroups of Native Americans on the Plains. Among the Plains tribes, both the Crow and Omaha were listed as archetypes among the six kinship systems devised by Louis Henry Morgan in 1871 (*Systems of Consanguinity and Affinity of the Human Family*). Most of the Western tribes fit into one or the other of these patterns to a greater or lesser extent.

Along the river bottoms of the Mississippi-Missouri river drainage system in the eastern and middle plains lived sedentary village dwelling farmers such as the Hidatsa, Mandan, Omaha, Kansa, Missouri, and others. Scattered in various other plains locations lived the "foot nomads," such as the ancestors of the modern Blackfoot, Comanche, Kiowa, and various Shoshone nations. In the western plains, groups moved toward the mountain valleys and shifted from nomadic hunting and gathering to more fixed-base hunting of rabbits and deer, while the eastern groups turned to a mixed economy with far more dependence on vegetal foods and small game. With the coming of the horse, some among the best-known Plains hunters, such as the Cheyenne, Arapaho, Crow, and Dakota— relative latecomers to the Plains—abandoned their settled agricultural ways of life for one of nomadic buffalo hunting and, as was the case among the southern Plains dwellers, raiding the towns of the native peoples of the southwestern agricultural area. It is to this extent only that the tribes of the Great Plains can be described as being part of a buffalo or horse culture, or those of the Desert Southwest can be described as a pueblo culture.

The development of a horse culture among the Plains peoples can be directly associated with the reintroduction of horses to the North American continent in the 16th century by the Spanish. There is no doubt that the Plains tribes quickly developed a remarkable ability with horses and that their way of life quickly became rooted in a *horse culture* that was in full bloom in the Old West Era. There were three primary uses among the Indians for horses: as riding animals during the hunt, as a tactical weapon of advantage in warfare, and as a burden bearer in moving camps. Indians did not plow, but their warriors were among the finest light cavalry in the history of the world.

It should be remembered that the horse culture did not immediately make inroads into the vast entirety of the West. Its adoption was slowed by the availability of appropriate animals and the willingness of the tribes of the southern Plains to trade breeding stock, especially stallions, to the north. Consequently, a Blackfoot born on the plains of Canada in the 1720s might have seen the first horse acquired by his people as a child and lived to see the horse culture become stabilized among them at the turn of the century. The native warrior reveled in his war stallion, and the Indians practiced no form of gelding (fixing). Indian warriors ridiculed white cavalry for riding geldings. Once present, the excellent range and abundant grasslands ensured a natural increase in the horse herds with relatively little care.

Horses had diffused northward from the Spanish settlements from which they were initially traded, stolen, or driven. Thereafter, many tribes turned to secondary horse-trading. The Pueblo revolt of 1680 against the Spanish estancias, rancheros, and missions was significant in that it threw almost all the horses in New Mexico onto the open Indian market. During the 18th century, the horse became a trading commodity among the tribes. Horses obtained by the Teton-Sioux from the Arikara were traded throughout the Dakota tribes. The Ute, and later the Comanche, became major suppliers to a secondary trading center among the Shoshone, while the Kiowa and Kiowa-Apache seem to have supplied horses as far away as the Upper Missouri. The Crow, who came late to the process, ultimately traded horses at a considerable profit all across the Plains. The Crow enjoyed stealing horses from their implacable enemy the Cheyenne. Cheyenne "Dog Soldiers," members of a warrior society that used Sirius (the Dog Star) as a totem, gladly retaliated. The profits to be had from horseflesh engendered a good deal of this intertribal raiding and rustling, and wealth, status, and marriage eligibility ultimately came to be measured in the number and quality of ones horses.

The chief cultural trait of the Plains nations in the period of the Old West was their single-minded dependence on the buffalo as a food source. These they had hunted since antiquity on foot with bow and arrows while disguised under a wolf-skin, or they drove whole groups of animals over cliffs to be killed or finished off with spears. The Native American bow was unsophisticated but effective as a tool for this purpose at a moderate range. Wolves were always prowling around the fringes of the herd, and the disguise allowed the hunter to get within the effective range of his weapons. Archeological evidence suggests that these practices may have ranged back at least 6000 years, but were somewhat displaced by light farming during the First Millennium AD and resurrected with the reemergence of the horse. The Pawnee were known to hunt buffalo from horseback before 1700. Nonetheless, when the first European fur trappers and traders moved up the Mississippi-Missouri river system, they found flourishing farming nations with rich and elaborate agricultural traditions.

In 1846, Francis Parkman observed a prairie teeming with buffalo, and he took the time to note how these abundant animals were hunted. Once among the buffalo, the mounted hunter dashes forward in utter recklessness and self-abandonment. He thinks of nothing, cares for nothing but the game. In the midst of the flying herd, where the uproar and the dust are thickest, he drops the reins, abandons his horse to its furious path, and lets fly the arrow, the lance, or the bullet. The wounded buffalo springs at his enemy; the horse leaps violently aside. The buffalo commonly continues his flight, but if the shot is well directed it soon stops. For a few moments it stands still, then totters and falls heavily upon the prairie. A practiced and skillful hunter, well mounted, could sometimes kill five or six cows in a single chase.[18]

It is important to remember that the Plains nations were striking exceptions to the general trend of tribal degradation, depopulation, and cultural deprivation following European and American contact. They had become prosperous and powerful under the influence of white trade and the expanded availability of firearms, and were able to offer the most effective armed resistance of any Native Americans to being conquered by the spreading white westward advance. In the immediate post-Civil War Era the northern Cheyenne and Sioux dominated the northern Plains; the southern Cheyenne and Arapahoe ruled the central Plains; and the Kiowa, Kiowa-Apache, and Comanche roamed virtually unopposed over the southern Plains. Although all had fought against the American military during the Civil War period of tribal conquest and compression, they still controlled vast domains in 1866. Nonetheless, hemmed in by the ever-tightening bonds of ranches, farms, settlements, railroad lines, wagon roads, telegraph lines, and other marks of the white man's possession of what had been buffalo range, the free bands were being slowly strangled to death.

Exploration and Exploitation

Initially on the Plains, financial gain had served as a greater stimulus to white exploration than scientific inquiry, and fur trappers had widely ranged among the more than 4 million square miles of wilderness. The federal government saw what was happening and gave the buffalo and hide-hunters encouragement. As General Sherman remarked: "They have done ... more to settle the vexed Indian question than the entire regular army. ... They are destroying the Indians' commissary." As the century progressed, land speculators, railroad magnets, prospectors, and cattlemen came to dominate.

Nonetheless, much of what is known about this part of America and its inhabitants has come through the work of the naturalists, explorers, and artists/authors who visited there in the Antebellum Period. "Even in its most primitive stage a cosmopolitan strain ran through the American borderland: it was a vastly thinned-out back yard of the world at large, where men of all nations and stations might meet and mingle in the course of their adventures." These men traveled widely and lived for extended periods among the Indians, often in little known or uncharted regions, recording their impressions not only in the written word, but also in sketches, paintings, engravings, and lithographs. In the decades before the common use of the photographic camera, these artists made their images bristle with nervous energy and romantic fervor. In many cases, they captured actions and reactions on canvas that the slow acting photographic processes of the day were incapable of recording.[19]

An emigrant train composed of covered wagons preparing to leave from Manhattan, Kansas in 1860. Nearby Fort Riley protected the free state settlement from the violence visited upon other towns by pro-slavery factions during the "Bleeding Kansas" era.

The era of westward expansion marked by wagon trains and railways ultimately gave way to an equally vibrant era of exploitation. Moreover, a generally sparse population of average persons attempting to eke out a living created an area through which cattle rustlers, bandits, gamblers, claim jumpers, outlaws, and outright killers could steal their way into western legend. Yet the wide-open area also sheltered some of the West's most revered characters: explorers, lawmen, soldiers, builders, missionaries, and political figures. Mostly the population was composed of hardworking, honest, self-reliant, and God-fearing persons (laborers, farmers, storekeepers, miners, ministers, and their families) who left little behind them but descendants of the same true-tested metal and high caliber of character.

Despite the magnificence of its scope and the extravagance of its style, Chicago's Columbian Exposition of 1893 was unable to capture fully all aspects of American life.

Many people felt that the West had been slighted since the Chicago exposition had emphasized industrial growth then concentrated in the East. Consequently official representatives were sent from the larger cities in the trans-Mississippi region to St. Louis in 1894 to form the Trans-Mississippi Commercial Congress—the first step leading to the Trans-Mississippi Exposition of 1898 in Omaha. Of the forty-five states in the Union in 1898, twenty-eight took part in the exposition including all nineteen western states and three territories. The city takes its name from a terrain feature, which is actually on the *west* bank of the Missouri River north of Omaha. On that bluff in 1804, Indians had met with the Lewis and Clark expedition. Opening at the time that it did—at the end of a decade of depression emphasized by the Panic of 1893—the exposition had wide grass-roots support, and the crowds were good despite official fears that the Spanish-American War would cut into the response of the populace. The exposition provided a showcase for the West, publicizing the region's resources, natural wonders, and safety. The fair brought to public attention how vast was the wealth yielded by a section of the country that had once been previously written off as barren.

The Frontier Army

The U.S. Army after the Civil War was the subject of the usual peacetime debates over its size—and therefore appropriations, its role, and its means of attaining and maintaining its professionalism. Being the enforcer, not the creator, of national policy, the army faced two major assignments in 1866—policing the South during Reconstruction, and maintaining order on the frontier. Both inevitably brought severe criticism from those opposed to the policies and from those whose lives were most directly affected.

The role of the frontier army was varied—to build and garrison forts; to drive white buffalo hunters and squatters from Indian reservations; to provide escorts for army paymasters and the U.S. mails; to maintain civil order; to supervise the distribution of rations to reservation Indians and to prevent theft by corrupt agents; to prevent smuggling of contraband liquor onto reservations; to protect miners and railroad construction crews; to prevent attacks on stage lines, railroads, or telegraph agencies; to protect visiting dignitaries, politicians, and peace commissioners; to bring recalcitrant Indians into reservations, and to engage in combat those who refused.

For all soldiers, life in the frontier army was difficult. When the *Army and Navy Journal* asked its readers to contrast mid-winter service in Montana, Dakota, and Idaho or mid-summer campaigning in Texas, New Mexico, and Arizona with anything known during the Civil War, respondents forcefully replied that the Civil War was a mere picnic when compared to service on the frontier. The truth of this assertion can be seen by examining the material surroundings of the frontier regular—his weapons, food, clothing, housing, and medical care; his duties both in garrison and in the field; and the harsh discipline to which he was subjected.

During the years after the Civil War, firearms had undergone a number of significant changes that speeded up the loading and firing sequence. Consequently, accuracy and speed became expectations rather than mere training objectives. This made competitive shooting–both amateur and professional–more exciting for both the participants and any spectators. Outstanding among the many sharpshooters that put on exhibitions of their skills was Annie Oakley. She was the finest woman sharpshooting entertainer of all time, and may have been the most famous woman to appear in American Wild West shows. Only her bigger-than-life employer, Buffalo Bill Cody, was more famous.

Note: Concerns over poor marksmanship abilities exhibited by recruits during the Civil War caused veteran Union officers Col. William C. Church and Gen. George Wingate to form the National Rifle Association (NRA) in 1871 for the purpose of promoting and encouraging shooting on a "scientific" basis. This was the first civilian organization of its kind in the world. Church and Wingate emphasized the study of ballistics, gunpowder chemistry, and marksmanship. In 1872, with financial aid from New York State, the NRA purchased a farm on Long Island to build a rifle range. Creed Farm (Creedmoor) was the site of the first National Rifle Matches until the crowds forced the NRA to move them to Sea Girt, New Jersey. In 1907, the extremely popular matches were again moved to Camp Perry, Ohio, a much larger location capable of supporting the crowds. They are still held there.

2. Going Armed in the West

Baseball is not our national sport ... shooting is and always will be.

—Cliff Robertson, Actor
The Great Northfield Minnesota Raid (1972)

Residents of the rural West seem to have shared a common grit: a way of being born of the wilderness, nursed on freedom, raised in intimate contact with the natural world. Both the early West's lawbreakers and those appointed to be lawmen were generally rugged, earthy individualists. Both were quick to resort to the decisiveness of gunplay and to ignore the finer points of the law for the broader precincts of justice.

Scholars have established that the Old West was not as violent as most movies and novels would suggest. Murder was not a daily, weekly, or even monthly occurrence in most small towns or farming, ranching, or mining communities. Most data that historians have gathered are preliminary, based on a single source such as newspapers, legal records, or official statistics, rather than on multiple sources. Still, homicide rates in the West were not extraordinarily high by the standards of the rest of the United States and the Western world in the nineteenth century.

For instance, the adult residents of Dodge City faced a homicide rate of at least 165 per 100,000 adults per year between 1875 and 1885, meaning that 0.165 percent of the population was murdered each year—between a fifth and a tenth of a percent. That may sound small, but it can be made to appear large to a criminologist. Yet there were not 2000 persons in Dodge City during this period, meaning that there were less than 3 killings in a decade! It can also be estimated, however, that there was only a 1-in-200 chance of homicide for all the Western cattle towns, less than 97 per 100,000 adults per year, if the five largest cattle towns studied to date were typical. As of 2015, Detroit has the second highest murder rate in the United States at 43.5 per 100,000, and with a population of 700,000 this represents more than 300 actual murders. St. Louis (population of 316,000) now has the highest murder rate at 49.9 murders per 100,000. Yet the populations of these cities are in the hundreds of thousands, meaning that scores of persons are killed each week. Modern murder rates vary greatly depending on the neighborhood in question, and do not include non-fatal violent incidents. In Detroit, for instance, the violent crime rate for one year is presently 2,000 per 100,000 persons.

Historically the term gunfighter or gunman referred to those who had gained a reputation of being dangerous with firearms and had previously participated in a number of gunfights and shootouts. Hundreds of western films have etched the image in the American cultural psyche of two gunfighters facing off on a dusty main street. Out come their revolvers, they fire and only one walks away. In reality, more missing took place then hitting, and more wounding took place than killing; but many participants later died of their wounds due to the poor availability of proper medical care.

Most commonly, gunfights broke out spontaneously to settle arguments, to exact revenge for some perceived slight, or for no good cause at all. There were very few "High Noon" moments. Compounding the violence were numerous lynchings (many due to racial or ethnic hatred); impatient citizens unwilling to wait for the decision of a legal process; too much alcohol and gambling; and a goodly number of blood feuds.

Gunfighters rarely took undue risks, and usually weighed their options before confronting another well-known gunman. This respect for one another is why most famous gunfights were rarely between two or more well-known antagonists. Today, the term "gunslinger" is now more or less used to denote someone who is quick on the draw with a handgun. Only a handful of historically known gunslingers were considered to be fast, but several gunmen were noted for being cold-blooded and businesslike employing shotguns and rifles. The usual winner of an encounter was the man who took his time and kept his emotions in check. Gunfighters ranged among different occupations including lawman, outlaw, exhibitionist, and duelist, but are more commonly synonymous to a hired gun that made a living with his weapons in the Old West.

The Gunfight at the O.K. Corral made legends of Wyatt Earp, Doc Holliday, and the Outlaw Cowboy gang, but they were relatively minor figures before that conflict ensued. Some gunslingers, such as Bat Masterson and Bill Hickok, actively engaged in self-promotion; others like Jonathan R. Davis and Elfego Baca had fame thrust upon them.

In a well-documented Old West gunfight resulting in the most kills by one person in a single event, Jonathan R. Davis took down eleven bandits single-handedly on 19 December 1854. Unknown to Davis and his companions, a band of robbers was lying in wait in the canyon brush near the trail. Captain Davis, a veteran of the Mexican War, later described himself as being "in a fever of excitement at the time." Unfazed, he stood his ground, pulling out both pistols and firing a barrage at the charging outlaws. He shot down seven assailants, one after another. But with his two Colt revolvers empty he dispatched the remaining four badmen with his Bowie knife. Several of the bandits were members of the Sydney Ducks gang. The shootout was witnessed by a group of miners, who buried the bodies of the dead in a shallow mass grave.[20]

This photograph purports to be of Captain Jonathan Davis.

In 1884 in Frisco, New Mexico, a cowboy named Charlie McCarty was celebrating the good life with a shooting spree inside a saloon. The Irish saloon owner named Bill Milligan requested Elfego Baca, a Mexican-American who was running for Socorro

County Sheriff, to disarm McCarty and arrest him. Lacking a formal jail, Baca held McCarty in an adobe house belonging to another Hispanic man. In no time, word of the ethnically charged arrest began to spread to the outlying ranches. The next day, some 80 cowboys surrounded the house and demanded McCarty's release. When Baca refused, the cowboys began firing. For the next 33 hours, Baca survived by lying prone on the sunken dirt floor and returning fire from the crevices between the wooden slabs. When the dust cleared, the unwounded Baca had killed four cowboys and wounded eight. Baca was tried for murder but acquitted after the bullet-ridden door of the house was entered as evidence. It had over 400 bullet holes in it.

Singular battles like these have long served as a symbol for the power of the lone individual, standing up against overwhelming odds for what he or she happens to believe is right. For the lay historian, the odds Baca faced evoke images of actor Gary Cooper in the film *High Noon*. It was this shootout that earned Baca his lifelong reputation as a tough hombre, a reputation that followed him throughout his years as a flamboyant criminal lawyer, school superintendent, district attorney, and American diplomat during the convoluted Mexican revolution.[21]

Much of the time, it would be difficult to tell who had "won" a gunfight for several minutes, as the black powder smoke from the pistols cleared the air. Black powder was the only propellant for guns from the 13th century until 1886 when the French developed the first usable smokeless powder. Bullets were usually of soft lead. The weapons seem to have been reliable if properly maintained. Jonathan Davis fighting with two cap and ball revolvers was able to dispatch more than a half dozen attackers with as many shots. Nonetheless, the firearms, bullet designs, and metals technologies from the 1860s through the 1880s weren't what they are today.

Elemental lead has long been held as an ideal bullet material, as it is readily available, easily formable, extremely dense, uniform, and soft enough to expand on contact. Pure lead maintains a uniformity and lack of brittleness (molecular cohesion) that has always made it an ideal bullet material. Soft lead requires great care in molding, seating, and handling, however. By swaging the lead, the hidden voids and uneven mass distribution problems of cast lead cores can be overcome. The shoulder busting conical .58 caliber rifle bullet used in the Civil War still has a ballistic coefficient comparable today to many known metal jacketed bullets even in smaller conical calibers.

Store-bought handgun cartridges were nearly laughable by modern standards. Even at their best the .38 caliber often used 150-grain conical bullets and the .44 used 200-grain bullets propelled by 18 and 20 grains of black powder, respectively. The precision with which these were produced, however, insured a standard level of performance that was often missing in hand loaded rounds. Muzzle velocities might vary as much as 10 percent due solely to the compression of the powder in the cylinder causing many shooters to load their weapons to the maximum. For its size and weight, however, nothing was so deadly as the round ball of pure lead when driven at fairly good velocities.

Samuel Fletcher who fought in the Civil War with the 2nd Illinois Cavalry claimed that the round ball fired from a hand loaded percussion revolver dropped enemy cavalrymen much better and took all the fight out of them, whereas the pointed bullet at times would only wound and leave them fighting. It has been suggested that the round ball's low sectional density made it behave somewhat like a modern expanded hollow point. Major R.E. Stratton of the 1st Texas Cavalry claimed, "While the big Dragoon was slower for quick-draw work, once you had it in your hand it was the best cavalry pistol of all." It would drop a horse as easily as a man with its .44 caliber round ball and 50 grains of black powder.[22]

This original package of .45 revolver ammo from 1874 clearly shows 30 grains of Black Powder behind a 250 grain conical bullet.

In regards to handguns, anything larger or heavier than the Colt Single Action Army was simply too unwieldy for belt carry. The single action mechanism needed to be cocked before each shot, but this generally led to better precision in terms of aim than the double action, which cocked and fired with a simple pull of the trigger. The single action was also thought to point more intuitively. Due to the force needed to actuate the hammer from its rest position, double actions tended to transfer all of their recoil straight back into the web of the hand, while single actions had a propensity to exhibit barrel rise and were designed in a manner that caused them to roll upward in the hand. Too heavy a finger on the trigger tended to pull the shot down and left from the point of aim. Caliber choice in this discussion is a moot point as either configuration (Dragoon or belt revolver) can be chambered in a significantly powerful caliber. The best one was often a matter of personal preference.

The primary reason for muzzle rise is the same for nearly all firearms. The centerline of the barrel is above the center of contact between the shooter and the firearms' grips or stock. The recoil from the bullet being fired and the propellant gases exiting the muzzle should ideally act directly down the centerline of the barrel. If that line of force is above the center of the shooter's hand, a rotational force causes the firearm to rotate, and the muzzle end to rise upwards. The upward rotation is imparted by the fact that most firearms have the barrel mounted above the center of gravity. Reducing the vertical distance between the barrel and the point of grip and adding more ergonomic contact points, such as a buttstock, can help to reduce muzzle rise. When the Thompson Submachine Gun first entered production as the M1921, its rapid fire and energetic .45 ACP caliber bullets caused it to rise in the extreme in two dimensions when fired in automatic mode. For a right-handed user, the muzzle tended to move up and to the left. Thompson had intended the weapon as an automatic "trench-broom" to sweep enemy troops from the trenches, filling a role for which the Browning Automatic Rifle (M1918 a.k.a. BAR) had been proven ill-suited. In 1926, the Cutts Compensator (a recoil brake) was offered as an option for the M1921.

Firearms are associated with the Old West more than with any other era of American history. Firearms were the primary tools for hunting and for self-defense against hostile elements on the American frontier. Initially, their efficiency was severely limited by the fact that the majority had to be reloaded after each shot. Until recent years when automatic handguns spewing dozens of bullets per minute are most closely associated with inner city street gangs and drug dealers, the six-shooter has been an iconic symbol of the American West and of individual self-reliance.

All modern firearms are, in reality, heat engines of Victorian design. They burn a fuel within them to produce a momentary emission of extreme heat and high-pressure gases. The bullet exhibits its highest velocity at the moment of its release from the barrel. The energy carried by the bullet is usually referred to as the kinetic energy. However, as with all heat engines, not all of the energy released by the burning of the fuel is transferred to the intended work function. The bullet carries only about 30 percent of the potential energy of the powder charge, which is in fact a respectable efficiency ratio for a firearm. Other functions account for the 70 percent of the energy that has been effectively lost, the bulk of which will have been used to heat up the barrel, the bullet, and cartridge case or released as muzzle blast. Rifle barrels are longer and more robustly constructed than pistol barrels and are designed to withstand far higher pressures than their pistol or shotgun counterparts. As a consequence the velocity of a rifle bullet is likely to be two or possibly three times that of an equivalent pistol bullet or shot charge.[23]

The guns used in the Old West were durable and powerful. When fired, the lead balls had a muzzle velocity of about 900 feet per second. From a range of 16 yards, a 140-grain bullet from a .44 caliber Colt Army revolver could penetrate several white pine boards, each ¾ inches thick, separated by one inch of dead space between them. The less massive .36 caliber round lead ball of the Colt Navy weighing 80 grains at a velocity of 1,000 feet per second is comparable to the modern .380 auto pistol cartridge in power. Today this is considered by some a minimum self-defense round, but only in comparison to the energetic and highly technical rounds available to modern shooters.

Loading and using a firearm in the 19th century was no simple matter. Cap and ball shooters had to force a lead ball into the several firing chambers of the cylinder. They often placed a lubricated wad between balls and powder, or, alternatively, packed lard or a bore lubricant at the mouth of each chamber in an attempt to prevent powder in an adjacent chamber from being ignited when the gun was fired, which is commonly known as a chain fire. Onto the nipple that was screwed and vented into the rear of the combustion chamber was placed a copper ignition cap containing the detonating composition, made of three parts of chlorate of potash, two of fulminate of mercury and one of powdered glass.

The process made reloading in a tactical situation virtually impossible, and caused shootists to carry multiple weapons in a loaded and ready condition. Although much of the result can be attributed to bravado, a reload in the Old West was reaching for another gun. For this reason many extant photographs of Westerners brim with multiple firearms.

These often included two massive revolvers, a pocket revolver, a vest pocket derringer, and, of course, a knife. Always carry a knife. It never runs out of bullets. (Rule Number 9).

The late 19th century was a very active period in firearm and cartridge development, and experimentation led to improvements. The most common nominal pistol calibers were .31, .36 and .44, but almost any size bullet might be fired in anger from the hundreds of private weapons carried in the Old West. A change from black powder to smokeless propellants late in the 19th century produced a marginal improvement in velocity as well as producing much less corrosive residue when fired. ***The pressure curve of the smokeless powder, however, is very different from that of black powder, and the two are not interchangeable.*** There is historic evidence that 19th century revolvers were often loaded with black powder to maximum capacity, and they did sometimes fail as a result. This is mostly attributed to the inconsistent metallurgy available at the time. It is of interest to note that in the black-powder period most powder charges were measured out by volume, both during the muzzle-loading period and during the early period of reloading cartridge ammunition. Disaster overcame people when first trying the new smokeless powders, which of course required considerably smaller charges to produce the same ballistic effect. Charges thrown by conventional powder measures resulted in burst guns, injury and sometimes death. (See Appendix 1)

It will be seen that the modern-style of handgun, shotgun and rifle cartridges paralleled the need for better firearms in the Old West. Firearms metallurgy has consistently improved from the end of the 19th century through the present day. The entire world recognizes that the topic of firearms history is replete with controversies and populated with many schools of thought and anecdote. Lacking any decisive or pivotal change, much of what follows will summarize a continuum of technological advances derived from reputable sources, and the reader should refrain from complaints about small differences in bullet mass, muzzle velocity, or the exact date of such-and-such advance. Get over it! If you know so much, write your own book.

Tests conducted by the U. S. Army with handguns in 1876 and again in 1898 provided surprising indications of the accuracy of Old West weapons. The .45 caliber Colt Single Action Army revolver turned in average groups of 3.1 inches at 50 yards, and in the later trials a Colt Peacemaker shot groups of 5.3 inches at 50 yards and 8.3 inches at 100 yards. In a recent controlled experiment a Colt Model 1851, like the ones used by Wild Bill Hickok, proved capable of putting three .36 caliber bullets in a 3 inch group at 25 yards. A Colt Model 1873 Single Action Army, like the ones used by Doc Holliday, Jesse James, and Billy the Kid, placed three rounds in a 3.5-inch group. A Colt Model 1860 Army percussion revolver, common in the Civil War, shot a three round 5-inch group. These results are very impressive, particularly in view of the age of the guns.

These period observations and recent tests make it readily apparent that frontier handguns were both precisely made and capable of real accuracy. The average velocities measured, however, had deviations from the mean that where as large as 100 fps. This last factor may have been due in large part to differences in powder compression. Generally, black powder cartridges were filled to the maximum volume of the case or cylinder leaving just enough room to properly seat the bullet. Generally velocities *averaged* from 700 to 900 feet per second, depending on powder quality, charge, and bullet weight. *All references to velocity that follow are given with these considerations in mind.*[24]

Smith and Wesson had purchased the American patent rights for cartridge-loaded weapons granted to Rollin White in 1855. These patents prevented their competitors at Colt from producing cartridge weapons in America, but other manufacturers produced them in Europe. Many well-known companies were ordered to cease manufacture because of patent infringement, among them Allen & Wheelock, Moore Patent Firearms, L.W. Pond, and E.A. Prescott. A few companies became licensees. Approximately 4300 revolvers were made under the Rollin White Arms name, most of which were then sold to or through Smith & Wesson to keep up with demand. After the patents ran their course in 1869, a number of Colt 1851 (and 1861 Navy) Revolvers were converted or newly made to fire .38 rimfire or centerfire cartridges, the *Colt Model 1851 Richards-Mason Conversion* by the Colt factory.

Muzzle loading rifles and cap and ball revolvers could fire any soft lead bullet that could be forced down the barrel or into the chamber with a modicum of relative safety. Breechloaders and cartridge handguns forced to fire oversized bullets—not so much. Makers of early cartridge arms had to invent methods of naming their cartridges, since no established convention then existed. Early on the Spencer Repeating Arms company named its cartridges based on the chamber dimensions, rather than the bore diameter, with the earliest cartridge called the "No. 56 cartridge," indicating a chamber diameter of .56 inches. The bore diameter varied considerably from .52 to .54 inches. The most common of the calibers used an undersized .50-inch hollow-base bullet, issued as a 56-50. Other schemes, that appeared similar to this, actually measured entirely different characteristics.

The .45-70, .38-40, and .32-20 were designated by bullet diameter in hundredths of an inch and a standard black powder charge in grains. This scheme was far more popular in America and was carried over after the advent of early smokeless powder cartridges. At the time Black Powder was measured by volume. Modern smokeless powders are measured by weight. Metric diameters for small arms refer to both bullet and cartridge dimensions and are usually expressed with an "X" between the diameter and the length; for example, 7.62×51 NATO. This indicates the bullet diameter is 7.62mm, loaded in a case 51mm long. Moreover, the means of measuring a rifled bore varies, and may refer to the diameter between the lands or between the grooves of the rifling.

Common sense would suggest that the numbers related to caliber have something to do with size and that they are precisely correct, but this is not the exact case. The caliber is specifically describing the width (diameter) of the slug portion. Caliber does not refer to the length or power of the bullet (in most cases), but simply the largest diameter of the bullet. Even today, bullet diameters vary greatly with the nominal caliber of many weapons, but soft lead is generally forgiving within certain limits when squeezed through a steel gun barrel. The tolerances seem to be on the order of a few thousandths (.003 or .004) of an inch. The most common bullet, the .22 caliber, varies depending on the manufacturer and intended use, between .220 and .224 inches. The most common handgun round, a .38 caliber spans .355 to .359 inches with the .357 Magnum sitting quite in the middle, and the .45 caliber from .451 to .454 inches. The "inches" measurements are considered part of the "Imperial System" of measurement instituted in Great Britain and retained by some of her former colonies – the most prominent of which is the U.S.A. Today, there remains a mix of metric measurements in millimeters (mm) and of Imperial measurements in inches. Each round has its own unique history and each gun its proper ammunition or sets of ammunition.[25]

The .38 Special, for example, was developed from the .38 Short Colt, which was designed for use in converted .36-caliber cap-and-ball Navy revolvers. These .36 caliber revolvers actually fired a slug that had a 0.357-inch diameter (rounded to .36 at the time). However, these revolvers had cylindrical firing chambers of approximately 0.374-inch diameter (rounded to .38). To make up for the difference, the original slug had a bit of a lip (or heal) at the bottom making it slightly wider to match the diameter of the bullet casing. As the round was perfected and revolvers were developed to specifically fire the new .38 Special round, the name .38 stuck while the actual size of the slug never changed from the 0.357-inch. The .38 Special can be fired from a revolver chambered in .357, but not the reverse as the Magnum cartridge will not fit in a chamber made for a .38 Special, and it develops over twice the peak pressure of the .38 Special.[26]

3. Historic Handguns

Abe Lincoln may have freed all men, but Sam Colt made them equal.
—An Old West Adage

Samuel Colt was an American inventor and industrialist from Hartford, Connecticut. In 1847, he founded Colt's Patent Fire-Arms Manufacturing Company and made the mass production of the revolver commercially viable. This was the successor corporation to Colt's efforts since 1836. At just 22 years old, he had proved himself to be a savvy businessman and promoter, but slow sales forced him to turn his attentions elsewhere. Colt's first two business ventures—producing firearms in Paterson, New Jersey, and making underwater mines for the Navy—ended in disappointment.

Nonetheless, no name was ultimately more closely associated with 19th century handguns. The Colt revolver was the gun (one of several) touted as the one that tamed the West; yet Colt never claimed to have invented the revolver. Rather, he envisioned that all the parts on every Colt gun would be interchangeable, made by machine, and later assembled by hand. Without a factory, Colt turned to Eli Whitney who had "first" envisioned manufacturing of this type for military muskets. Precise tolerances of this sort had not before been attempted on the much smaller and more intricate revolving handgun. At one exhibit, and to the amazement of the viewers, Colt disassembled ten guns and reassembled ten guns using all the different and unsorted parts from the original weapons.

By the end of 1837, the Colt Arms Company had made over 1,000 weapons, but there were few sales. However, Colt's business expanded rapidly after 1847, when the Texas Rangers ordered 1,000 revolvers during the American war with Mexico. Thereafter, his revolvers were the standard by which virtually all other handguns were measured in the 19th century. By 1856, Colt was producing 150 weapons a day. As the Old West adage suggests, the revolver was the great equalizer on the frontier.

The Colt Paterson

The Model 1836 Colt Paterson .36 caliber revolver was the first commercial repeating firearm employing a revolving cylinder with multiple chambers aligned with a single, stationary barrel. This made it different from the multi-barreled revolving pepper-box weapons then appearing on the market. The Colt Paterson was a percussion gun using black powder, lead balls, and percussion caps for ignition. Single action with a five shot cylinder, the model as originally designed and produced, had no loading lever and no trigger guard. The trigger folded into the weapon and only became visible upon cocking the hammer, which process was repeated for each shot. This seriously increased the time between successive shots and forced the user to reestablish his grip for each firing. The unfluted cylinder of the Colt Paterson was "rebated," meaning that the rear of the cylinder was turned to a smaller diameter than the front. The actual dimensions of the ball (.375-.380 inch) allowed for a few mils of lead to be compressed in the cylinder to ensure a tight fit. The user had to partially disassemble the revolver to re-load it. In 1839, a hinged loading lever and capping window became standard for new revolvers and was retrofitted to the older designs. So modified, the revolvers could be loaded without disassembly. Remarkably, the chambers could be left loaded for long periods with no deterioration of performance or corrosion of the metal. Unloading without firing was virtually impossible without disassembly of the weapon.

Compared to later models of a similar design the 1836 was ergonomically flawed, but the inclusion of a rifled barrel suggests that Colt intended the weapon to be accurate. The smaller versions of Colt's first revolvers are also called "Baby Patersons" by collectors and were produced first in .24 and .31 calibers, and later in .36 caliber, by means of further rebating the frame and adding a "step" to the cylinder to increase the chamber diameter. Civilian demand for the original .31 caliber revolver (approximate muzzle energy 68 ft-lbs) remained substantial even after introduction of the larger-bored .36 caliber Pocket Navy and Police Models due largely to their ease of concealment and negligible recoil.

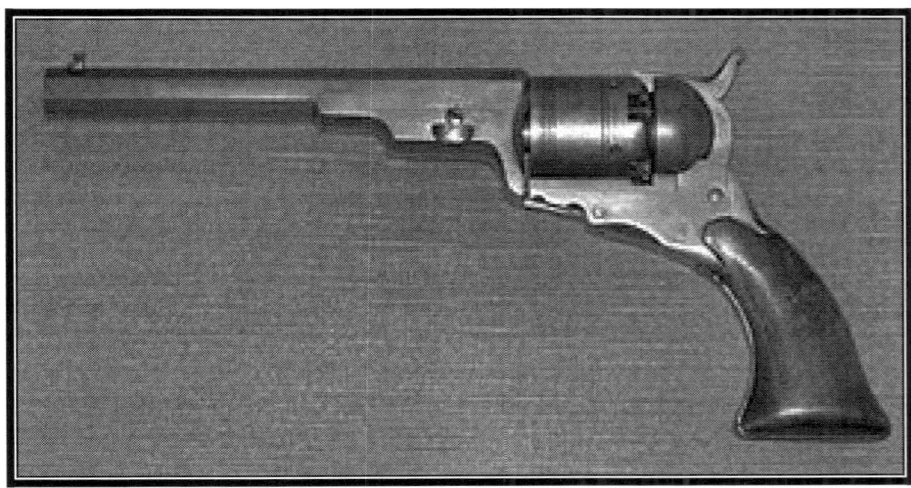

Model 1836 Colt Paterson [27]

The early Republic of Texas purchased 180 revolving shotguns and rifles as well as a large number of handguns from Colt. These revolvers were first used by Texas during the revolt against Mexico (c. 1836). The repeating handguns later became very popular with the Texas Rangers, providing them with sustained firepower against their adversaries. Prior to the use of multiple-shot revolvers, Indians had been able to draw the fire of single-shot weapons and would renew an attack before the guns could be re-loaded. In 1844, fifteen Rangers led by Captain Jack Hays first used the Colt Paterson and defeated a band of 80 Comanches at the battle of Walker Creek northwest of San Antonio. With the five-shot Paterson, the Texas Rangers changed forever the rules of engagement in frontier Indian fighting.

The reader should not misapprehend the power of these early revolvers. In general, .36 caliber black powder revolvers with an 80 grain ball (185 ft-lbs) compare favorably to modern .380 ACP (200 ft-lbs) and .38 S&W Long (207 ft-lbs) hollow point cartridges of 125 grains because of the BP ball's remarkable velocity (approximately 1000 fps), but they had about half the energy of the modern 9 mm (351 ft-lbs) of the same approximate diameter and mass moving at 1200 fps. In measuring muzzle energy, velocity is squared, meaning that a faster bullet generally has much greater energy than a slower one if their masses are equal. Reminder: *All other factors being equal*, a less massive bullet leaves the weapon at a greater velocity under the influence of equal amounts of gunpowder.

Colt Walker and Dragoon

In a joint venture between Samuel Colt and Captain Samuel Walker, the two men collaborated on a handgun named the Colt Walker (or Walker Colt). The revolver was chambered in .44 caliber with a 140 grain ball at almost 900 fps and produced about 400 ft-lbs of energy. The heavier bullet, ostensibly provided to allow the take down of enemy horses (140gr. vs. 80gr. ball of the .36 caliber), brings down velocity substantially between the .44 and .36 respectively. However, the larger .44 chamber allowed a greater load of powder. The Colt Walker was actually a .451-.454 caliber, but Colt wanted to continue the .44 naming convention popular at the time for advertising purposes.

Samuel Walker carried two of his namesake revolvers in the Mexican–American War. He was killed in battle in 1847 shortly after he had received them. He was struck from his horse by a shotgun round fired from a balcony and then run through with a lance. Fewer than 170 original Colt Walkers are known to exist and collectors have paid more than $100,000 for extant revolvers in good condition.

The death of Captain Samuel Walker at Huamantla in Mexico.

The original Colt Walker was quite powerful, and modern replicas firing modern FFFg black powder can produce energy levels in excess of 500 foot-pounds (average 480 ft-lbs). The original design at maximum matched the minimum ballistics of the modern .357 Magnum JHP, and until 1929 it was regarded as the most powerful revolver available. Yet almost 30 percent of the early Walkers issued to the military were returned due to rupture of the cylinders. Much of this may have been due to mishandling and overloading. Colt recommended no more than 50 grains of powder in each cylinder but 60 grains could be loaded under a well-seated bullet.

The excessive recoil on the Walker often caused the balls in the unfired cylinders to creep forward under the influence of inertia. This could "lock up" the cylinder at an inconvenient moment or cause a wide variation in performance. The use of oversized bullets (.45 ball in a .44 chamber) was meant to better secure the balls in place. Bullet creep was often an unrecognized threat even with muzzle loading long arms, especially those carried by the cavalry where the jostling of the horse often moved the bullet down the barrel if the weapon was carried muzzle down for an extended amount of time.

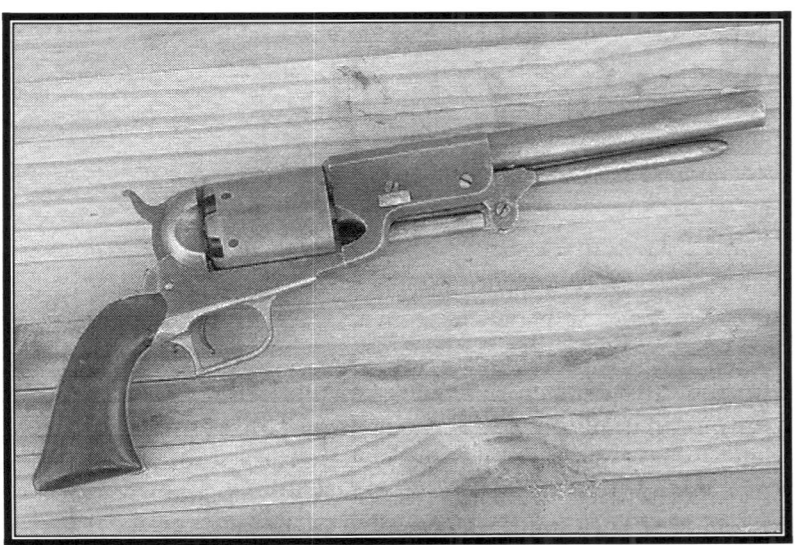

The Model 1846 Colt Walker [28]

Later revolvers of similar caliber were issued to the Army's "Dragoon" Regiments. The Colt Dragoon Revolver gained popularity among civilians in the Southwest where many had served in the Mexican-American War. The latter revolver was designed as a solution to numerous problems encountered with the Colt Walker. The Colt Dragoon Revolver had a comparatively shorter cylinder (thus preventing overloading the chamber) and held no more than 50 grains of powder under a well-seated bullet. The Colt Dragoon Revolver was produced with several variations between 1848 and 1860. Other variants included the Colt "1848 Pocket Pistol" now known as the Baby Dragoon.

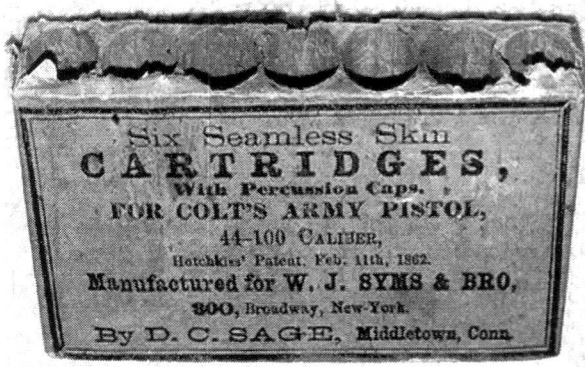

The seventh hole in this package of revolver cartridges was for a
paper twist containing percussion caps.

Encouraged by an ongoing military contract, Colt turned his eye toward the civilian market in 1848. Civilian pocket revolvers, such as the Wells Fargo or 1849 Pocket, were .31 caliber pistols that fit easily in a coat pocket. The spent priming caps on the smaller framed revolvers tended to jam up the gun more often then on the larger framed weapons. This was hardly a factor when shooting the larger frames, which chewed the spent caps up and spit them out more easily due to the increased mechanical advantage of the larger moving parts.

Just as better and more resilient steels allowed Colt to adapt a .44 cylinder to a .36 frame, it permitted the .31 caliber 1849 Pocket revolver to be upgraded to a .36 caliber. All the improvements in design of Colt revolvers were applied to the Dragoons as well as to the smaller models of Colt revolvers. Always the businessman, Colt persuaded the governor of the state of Connecticut to make him a lieutenant colonel and aide-de-camp in the state militia. With this rank, he toured Europe to promote his line of revolvers.

Colt Navy

The 1851 Navy Model was basically a larger .36 caliber version of the Pocket Model. It was a weapon sized to fit into a belt holster, as opposed to the saddle holsters generally called for by Colt's larger cavalry combat models. The development of stronger and more consistent metals allowed Colt and other manufacturers to lighten their weapons at mid-century without sacrificing safety. The Colt Walker weighed a hefty 4.5 pounds, the 1851 Navy only 2.6 pounds. Bill Hickok's favorite guns were a pair of Colt 1851 Navy Model (.36 caliber 260 ft-lbs) cap-and-ball revolvers, which he commonly carried thrust into a sash around his waist. He is supposed to have put a bullet in the heart of an opponent at 75 yards with this weapon.

While similar in design to the 44 Colt Army Model 1860, the lighter recoil of the 1861 Navy's 36 caliber (.375-.380 ball or conical) was preferred by some cavalry troopers in the Civil War. Other variants included the Colt Pocket Pistol marketed in California with success during the Gold Rush days. The Pocket Police had a fluted 5-shot cylinder, while most Army Models were unfluted, and held six shots. Between 1862 and 1873, Colt records document production of 19,000 of the Pocket Navies and over 20,000 Pocket Police revolvers. The revolvers of the so-called "Wells Fargo" series were designed for easy concealment, their most noticeable feature being the lack of a loading lever.[29]

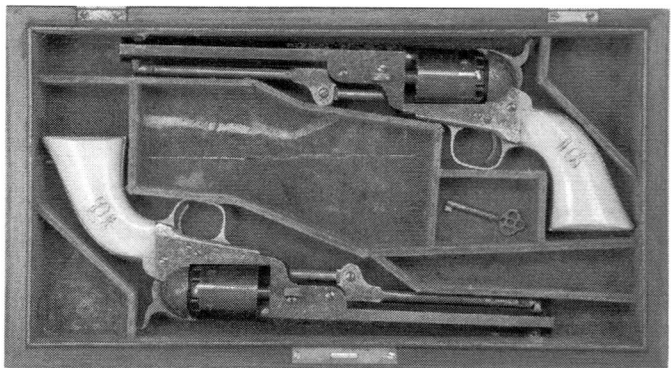

A presentation set of Colt Navy revolvers.

As the American Civil War approached, Colt supplied both the North and the South with firearms. In response to charges of disaffection, Colt was recommissioned as a full colonel by the state of Connecticut in 1861 in the 1st Regiment Colts Revolving Rifles of Connecticut, each man armed with the Colt revolving rifle provided by the manufacturer. The unit never took the field, and Colt was discharged on June 20, 1861 due to poor health. He died of an illness in January 1862, and his professional responsibilities were turned over to his brother-in-law, Richard Jarvis.

Remington Full-Frame Revolvers

Subsequently models and variations of percussion revolvers were manufactured by Eliphalet Remington & Sons in .31 (Pocket) .36 (Navy) or .44 (Army) caliber, and used during the Civil War. This was the beginning of a successful line of medium and large full frame pistols. The Remington revolver was a secondary, supplemental issue firearm for the Union Army until the Colt factory fire of 1864 produced a shortage of handguns. The Remington revolver owes its durability to the "top strap," solid-frame design. The design is stronger and less prone to frame stretching than the Colt revolvers of the same era. The top strap design was not previously thought possible because the "soft metal" of early cylinders often cause them to go "out of round" and threaten to jam while rotating—hence the open top style of the Colt. Stronger metals obviated this threat. Another innovative feature (first appearing in 1863) was "safety slots" milled between chambers on the cylinder. The milled slot positively secured the hammer between chambers for safe carry by preventing accidental cylinder rotation. These slots were advertised as eliminating the need to keep one cylinder unloaded making a six-shooter a true six shooter! Remington percussion revolvers were very accurate and capable of considerable power with muzzle velocities in the range of 550 to 1200 feet-per-second, depending upon the bullet size and charge loaded by the shooter.

Smith and Wesson

The production of metallic cartridges and breech loading revolvers eliminated the need for placing caps on the cylinder and packing powder and balls into the chambers. The first self-contained cartridge was the modern .22 caliber rimfire patented by Smith and Wesson in 1854. The small tip-up barrel S&W .22 revolver was a pathetic defensive weapon, and it was followed by a slightly more energetic .32 caliber cousin. Releasing the barrel latch and removing the cylinder easily reloaded both weapons.

These were followed by a slew of four-barrel micro-pepperbox guns designed by Christian Sharps around the small rimfire cartridges. Civil War soldiers often carried early rimfire revolvers as personal pocket weapons. Their use or effectiveness was minimal but they provided some feeling of added protection. As soldiers came to realize that their government issued weapons were reliable, most small "personal" handguns became a nuisance to carry and were sent home or traded and sold off. Following the Civil War, the little guns often served as traveler's companions on stagecoaches and trains. The homeowner and shopkeeper had one in the drawer for protection against itinerants and shoplifters. Despite the publicity given to the one- and two-shot Derringers, ladies of the evening and gamblers often preferred the compact little revolvers and pepperboxes.

There were thousands of inexpensive surplus cap and ball revolvers on the market in 1866. The Remington Army cartridge-conversions in 46 rimfire were the first large-caliber cartridge revolvers available after the war, beating even Smith & Wesson's .44 American to market by nearly two years (1868). Although Colt was convinced at the time that the percussion revolver would never be replaced, with the success of the cartridge revolver and the expiration of the Smith and Wesson patent, Colt Manufacturing turned its attention in 1871 to inexpensively converting cap and ball revolvers to cartridge revolvers for the Army.

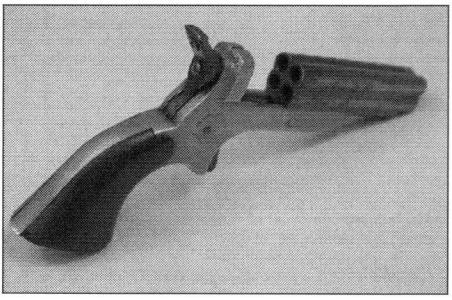

The 1859 C. Sharps .22 and .32 rimfire pepperboxes rotated the striker rather than the barrels. The cylinders slid forward as one piece to reload, but there was no spent case extractor.

Once again, almost any size bullet might be fired in anger from the hundreds of private weapons carried in the Old West. Thousands of pistols, sometimes advertised as "lifesavers," were carried in holsters, pockets and waistbands, but many were small rimfire cartridge weapons of .22 and .32 caliber of little power that proved useless except as a last means of defense. Of course, a small gun is better than no gun when the need arises. Loaded with a light 28-grain load of black powder and a 140-grain round ball, the .44 revolver rivals a modern .38 Special. Loaded with an average powder load of 35 to 40 grains it rivals the modern 9mm and .45 ACP. Loaded with 45 and 50 grains it starts to approach the power of the .357 Magnum of similar bullet weight.

Schofield Revolvers

The Smith & Wesson Model 3 was a single-action, cartridge-firing, top-break revolver produced by Smith & Wesson from circa 1870 to 1915. The so-called Schofield revolver was an improvement and up-grade of earlier top-break Single Action revolvers produced in the line of the legendary firearms company Smith & Wesson.

Immediately after the Civil War (circa 1868), the No. 3 Smith & Wesson revolver was chambered for the .44 S&W American cartridge, an anemic centerfire round developed by Smith & Wesson for use in the original, rather weak, top break No. 3 action. In 1870, the US Government ordered 1000 No. 3 revolvers in .44 American, but no further orders for No. 3 revolvers followed until the advent of the improved Schofield model five years later. Major Schofield's most significant improvement to the No. 3 revolver was a frame mounted, spring-loaded, stirrup-type latch replacing S&W's original barrel mounted latch. The .44 American cartridge's main claim to fame is that it was soon developed into the .44 Russian for use by the Imperial Russian Army, which ordered some 41,000 No. 3 revolvers with seven inch barrels in 1871. The .44 Russian proved to be a successful cartridge and when early smokeless powders were developed the .44 Russian case was lengthened and the .44 Special was born.

Like any single action revolver, the Schofield's hammer had to be manually cocked before the weapon could be fired. That is about its only similarity to the more popular Colt and Remington single action revolvers. There was no side loading gate or external ejector rod housing on a Schofield. Instead, S&W's single action was a top break design. It was the Schofield version that ensured the revolver's lasting fame.

The break-open design and spent case extractor made the Schofield easier to load and reload on horseback. The cylinder had a recess in its rear face, which was surrounded by a shoulder. In the base of this recess was an extractor star carried by the ejector rod.

The United States Army contracted a total of over 5000 Schofields with 7-1/2 inch barrel lengths. The Schofield No. 3 revolvers were widely used on the Western frontier and in the various Indian Wars (on both sides) in the US and Canada. A 1875 Smith & Wesson Schofield revolver was found at the Little Bighorn (1876) by a party of surveyors in 1883. This could have been an Indian gun but is much more likely to have belonged to an officer or scout.

The final evolution of the No. 3 was the "New Model Number Three," introduced in 1877. This incorporated additional improvements and replaced all previous models. This revolver represented the first real challenge on the military and civilian market to the Colt Single Action. In 1898, the Army sold as surplus their remaining Schofield revolvers. Wells Fargo & Company purchased many of these Army surplus Schofields, shortening their seven-inch barrels to a handier five inches for carry by their Agents.

Graceful and accurate the Schofield revolver was the choice of many gunslingers and entrepreneurs in the Old West. Perhaps the most famous of these was the outlaw Billy the Kid (William H. McCarty, Jr., a.k.a. William H. Bonney), who was known to prefer the No. 3. Others associated with the No. 3 at some point in their careers include Pat Garrett (who killed Billy), Jesse James, John Wesley Hardin, Wyatt Earp, Wyatt's brother Virgil and Annie Oakley.

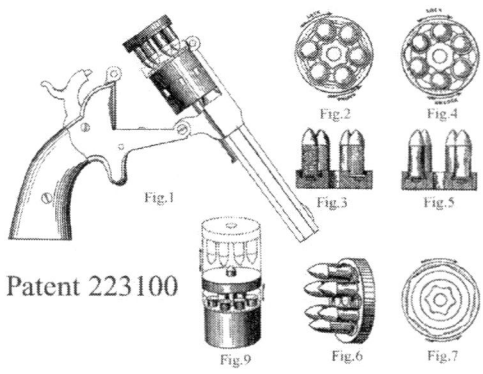

William H. Bell patented the first revolver speedloader in 1879. Bell's device was a simple metal disk with a rotating locking mechanism that held six revolver rounds.

A Word Concerning Fluting

In firearms terminology, fluting refers to the removal of material from a cylindrical surface, usually creating grooves. Fluted pistol cylinders began as a practical modification added to strengthen black powder revolvers similar to adding an arch to strengthen a structure, or forging the misnamed blood groove (fuller) in a sword blade. Each hand-loaded chamber produced different pressures depending on the amount, quality, and compression of the powder. The flutes equalized the pressure somewhat, helped to prevent cylinder oblation (going out-of-round), and allowed more reliable turning of the cylinder between the top strap and the bottom frame. Early revolvers without the top straps like the Colt were seldom fluted, but most later models were. Lowering the cylinder weight through fluting is also useful in reducing wear on the moving parts and helps keep the gun running in time (alignment of the chamber and barrel). While a fluted barrel may cool more quickly under a rapid firing, a non-fluted barrel will be stiffer and be able to absorb a larger amount of total heat at the price of additional total weight.

The introduction of multi-shot revolvers and rifles gave settlers and hunters a new and distinct advantage over the single shot belt pistols and long rifles of an earlier era. The newer models were generally unsophisticated, even if effective and innovative weapons. They produced lethal energies approximately equal to many 21st century handguns of similar size and caliber. Many shooters express surprise when cap and ball revolvers deliver amazingly precise and forceful hits on targets. Their surprise is often a product of their lack of familiarity with these weapon systems. The capacity of revolvers was normally six shots, though single to five shot pocket guns were common. The oddball LeMat revolver of Confederate fame held nine shots of .36 or .44 ball plus a separate 20- or 28-gauge shotgun barrel. A surplus of post-war small arms existed well into the second decade of the 20th century making them common possessions among the frontier population.

4. Historic Long Arms

Fads and Fancies

Not surprisingly, gun owners are often part of a "social gun culture" in which certain facts, trends, and fads circulate and evolve with time, some stirring intense loyalty among gun owners even when the realities suggest otherwise. One of the more interesting facts concerning the type of firearms being carried by lawmen and outlaws by the early 1900s was their modernity.

Tube fed repeaters such as the lever-action Spencer, Henry, and Winchester rifles gradually replaced the muzzleloaders and the single shot breechloaders of the Civil War. Evolved from the 1860 Henry rifle, Winchester rifles were among the earliest repeaters. No gun of the period shot more often or as reliably as did the Winchester—some models were capable of holding as many as 16 cartridges. The Model 1873 was particularly successful, being colloquially known as "The Gun that Won the West." Introduced to celebrate the American Centennial Exposition, the Model 1876 earned a reputation as a durable and powerful hunting rifle. Most popular of all was the Winchester lever-action Model 1894, a new design by John Browning widely adopted as a hunting rifle that saw production of over 6 million units before being discontinued in 2006.

A review of various articles and books suggests that Theodore Roosevelt had at least 20 Winchester rifles in his hunting collection. For Roosevelt, the combination of the fast working lever-action and the power of the new smokeless sporting cartridges made the Model 1895 the perfect rifle. "I have met plenty of men accustomed to killing wild turkeys and deer with small-bore rifles in the southern forests who, when they got on the plains and in the Rockies, were absolutely helpless," wrote TR. "The spice of danger, especially to a man armed with a good repeating rifle, is only enough to add zest to the chase, and the chief triumph is in outwitting the wary quarry and getting within range."[30]

For military purposes, these clearly traditional "American" weapons were usurped in turn by more advanced bolt-action rifles of the Spanish American War like the Norwegian Krag–Jørgensen (Springfield Model 1892–99) and the eminent German Mauser and its derivatives. The standard military issue US Krag was replaced beginning in 1903 with the introduction of the US M1903 Springfield rifle, which was essentially a copy of the Model 1898 (K98) Mauser's bolt and magazine systems, along with a higher-velocity .30-40 caliber cartridge (later reformulated as the .30-06). The interconnections between the Mauser and other bolt-action weapons of this period cannot be ignored both in terms of military and civilian uses. In particular, they introduced the concepts of vertical box magazine feeding, and in-line cocking, ignition, and ejection systems.

Examples of the bolt-action system can be dated as far back as the early 19th century notably to the Dreyse Needle Gun (c. 1836). From the late 19th century, all the way through both World Wars, the bolt-action rifle was the standard infantry firearm for most of the world's militaries. Ultimately almost every military agency turned to bolt-action rifles using a box magazine, a system that changed the face of warfare in the 20th century. Among the first of its kind to use a box magazine was the bolt-action M1885 Remington–Lee (a.k.a. US Navy Model 1885), arguably the most modern rifle in the world until the introduction of smokeless powder. It first appeared in 1879, manufactured by the Sharps

Rifle Manufacturing Company. Eventually Remington took over production and produced copies in .45-70 black powder.

The bolt-action Krag–Jørgensen with its side box magazine became the standard US issue weapon in 1893. Around 500,000 "Krags" in smokeless .30-40 caliber were produced at the Springfield Armory in Massachusetts from 1894 to 1904. Ironically, the iconic Krag rifle had the shortest service life of any standard-issue firearm in US military history. The Krag was phased out of service with the regular Army as M1903 Springfields became available, but it was issued for many more years with the National Guard and the Army Reserve, including service in World War I with rear-echelon troops and as a training arm. The Krag–Jørgensen was manufactured for almost 60 years in Norway.

The primary reason for the selection of the foreign-designed Krag by US authorities appears to have been its magazine design that was integral with the receiver into which several cartridges could be "dumped" at once with no need for precise placement. Shutting the magazine-door forced the cartridges to line up correctly inside the magazine. At the time of its adoption rapidity of fire was deemed to be of lesser importance in an era when current military fire control protocol still emphasized precise aimed fire and conservation of ammunition. The magazine with its cut off switch was looked upon as a reserve, to be used only when authorized by a commanding officer. The Krag design was also easy to "top off," and unlike most top-loading magazines, this could be done without opening the rifle's bolt. However, only one cartridge could be added to the magazine at a time. This magazine design became a distinct disadvantage once US soldiers encountered Spanish troops armed with the charger-loaded 1893 7mm Spanish Mauser in the Spanish–American War.

Compared to most other manually operated firearm actions, the bolt-action offered an excellent balance of strength allowing for more powerful cartridges, ruggedness, reliability, and potential accuracy, all with lighter weight and fewer moving parts than self-loading firearms. The major disadvantage was a slightly lower practical rate of fire than other manual repeating firearms, such as lever-action and pump-action firearms. In the Mauser-style turn-bolt action, for instance, the bolt handle must be rotated counter-clockwise, drawn rearward, pushed forward to chamber the round, and finally rotated clockwise back to lock the breech. In some formats the action is cocked on the opening of the bolt (as in the Mauser system) or the closing of the bolt (as in the Lee–Enfield system). This was much more complicated than the lever action of the Winchester, but the innate strength of the bolt allowed for higher pressures and greater muzzle velocities.

The German Mauser is often considered the epitome of this type of action, and its descendents have become the standard against which all such rifles are measured. The weapon was designed with a lot of thought. The bolt handle is securely attached to the bolt, for instance, and there are a couple of gas vent holes built into the bolt, so that if there is a rupture in the cartridge case or primer, the hot gases will vent out of the magazine hole instead of near the user's face. Bolt actions are more accurate than semi-automatic rifles, which is why hunters and military snipers still use them. When the cartridge is fired, the entire energy is devoted to propelling the bullet out of the rifle, unlike a semi-automatic or automatic weapon, where part of the energy is diverted to eject the old cartridge, auto-cock the weapon and load a new cartridge. Mausers and most other bolt actions were readily adapted as hunting rifles, which may help to explain the longevity of their wide popularity in the civilian market. Weapons made available through military surplus were often rechambered in larger rounds up to and including .50 caliber (12.7 mm) for the purpose of big game hunting.

Mauser designs were built for the armed forces of Germany (Prussia), but they were widely used elsewhere. The Mauser gained a deadly reputation among the Americans that faced it. The Spanish Army in Cuba used the 1893 Mauser against US forces and insurrectionist forces in Cuba and the Philippines. At the legendary Battle of San Juan Hill (1898), 750 Spanish regulars armed with Mausers significantly delayed the advance of 8,500 US troops armed with a mix of outclassed .30-40 Krag–Jørgensen bolt-action rifles and older single-shot, trapdoor Springfield rifles, inflicting 1,400 US casualties. The Krag officially entered US service in 1894, only to be replaced nine years later by the US Springfield M1903.

The Mauser's 7mm cartridge (2300 fps at 55,000 psi) produced 300 fps higher velocity and a resultant flatter trajectory over the .30 Army cartridges used in the US Krag–Jørgensen rifle. The initial smokeless loading of the .30 Army round increased the muzzle velocity in the M1896 Krag to 2,200 fps at 45,000 psi. However, once the new loading was issued, reports of cracked locking lugs on service Krags began to surface. In March 1900, the remaining stocks of this ammunition (some 3.5 million rounds) were returned to the arsenals, broken down, and reloaded back to the original 2,000 fps specification (and slightly less for the cavalry carbine version). This effectively extended the range of the Spanish defense and gave the Spanish Mauser a major advantage over the Krag that was issued to many US troops. In addition, it was noted that the Mauser's stripper clip system allowed the Spaniards to reload far more quickly than could be done with the Krag, whose magazine had to be loaded one round at a time.

Roosevelt had seen the awesome effect smokeless cartridges had on battlefield tactics in Cuba in 1898 when his men were subject to withering fire from the new Spanish Mausers. Roosevelt, himself carried a M1895 Winchester chambered for the .30 Army and a Model 1892 DA .38 Service Revolver in Cuba. It is also noted that TR presented M1895 Winchesters to all of the officers of the Regiment. The "Rough Riders," a collection of Western cowboys and Eastern blue bloods, officially known as the First U.S. Voluntary Cavalry, believed that their precise positions were being made known to the enemy from the clouds of white smoke surrounding them after firing. The round retained the "caliber-charge" naming system of earlier black powder cartridges, which may have led the soldiers to an incorrect assumption. As with the early .30-30 Winchester, it was the use of black powder nomenclature that may have led to the assumption that the .30-40 Krag was once a black powder cartridge, or it may have been actual smoke from other older black powder weapons (.45-70) issued among some state militias. The *New York Times* (16 August 1898) decried, "The nation which sends its troops on a modern battlefield with black powder is deliberately sacrificing them to its own ignorance, parsimony, and negligence."

The truth of these assertions cannot be verified, but it is certain that the US troopers soon found themselves under a steady stream of Spanish bullets fired from out of range of their own exposed positions. Roosevelt, feeling very excited, began to ride up and down the line urging the men forward. Seeing Roosevelt personally urging them forward, momentum quickly spread and finally the entire regiment was on the move, passing the lines of other American units. As the Americans reached the barbed wire fence line, it became apparent to the Spanish defenders that to avoid hand-to-hand combat, they must withdraw. About 10,000 rounds of Mauser ammunition was found in the captured trenches. Roosevelt's personal actions at the battle of San Juan Heights would win him the nation's highest military honor, the Congressional Medal of Honor. A US Army board of investigation was commissioned to make changes in American ordnance as a direct result of this battle.

The Model 1871 was the Mauser brothers' (Peter and Wilhelm) first rifle, but actual production of the weapon was given to government arsenals and large firms. Slightly modified versions of the German Mauser were widely sold to many other countries, initially firing bullets that would today be considered very large, typically 9.5mm to 11.5mm. Such large massive bullets were thought necessary due to the limitations of black powder, which hindered increased velocities. In 1886, the French Army introduced the Lebel Model 1886 rifle, which used a smokeless powder cartridge. Smokeless powder allowed smaller diameter bullets to be propelled at higher velocities, with accuracy to 1,000 yards, making most other military rifles obsolete. However, the magazine was tube fed and slow to reload. The Model 1893 was the first Mauser to use a staggered-row magazine, which permitted the magazine to be charged with less effort, fed cartridges more smoothly, and being completely enclosed by the stock, was almost impervious to damage.

Germany was also the primary supplier of guns to the Boers in their struggles with Britain in southern Africa. The most common of these, and the one that was to become a symbol of the Boer struggle against British imperialism, was the Model 1893/1895 Mauser chambered for the 7mm cartridge. In 1896, the Boers ordered 70,000 Mauser rifles and carbines. With this rifle the Boers showed the military authorities of the day the true potential of the new small-bore, smokeless powder rifle with an average velocity of almost 2300 fps. The strong following enjoyed by surplus military Mausers, especially the K98 7.92mm (by far the most successful of the Mauser designs), is partly a testament to their reliability and quality of manufacture.

The US Springfield Model 1903 was a 5-round magazine fed bolt-action repeating rifle used primarily during the first half of the 20th century. The integral magazine could be top-loaded from a 5-cartridge stripper clip or fired one cartridge at a time with the magazine feed switched off. Each stripper clip contained 5 cartridges, and standard issue consisted of 12 clips carried in a cloth bandolier. The adoption of the M1903 was preceded by nearly 30 years of struggle largely retarded by politics. The M1903 not only replaced the various versions of the Army's Krag, but also the Lee Model 1895 and M1885 Remington-Lee used by the United States Navy and the United States Marine Corps, respectively, and all remaining single-shot trapdoor Springfield Model 1873s. It was the standard US service weapon used on the Mexican border and in WWI. By January 1905, over 80,000 of these rifles had been produced. The weapon was then fine-tuned as the early versions were characterized by a so-called "fourth round hang up." Ultimately there would be 1.3 million produced among all its variants.

With the .30-06 cartridge, the M1903 Springfield was capable of an outstanding muzzle velocity of 2800 fps and an effective range of 1000 yards. In this respect it set the standard for most infantry rifles of the Second World War. Officially replaced by the venerable semi-automatic 8-round M-1 Garand in 1937, the M1903 remained in service as an issue infantry rifle to support elements and reserves as the US entered WWII in

1941 because the Army was initially without sufficient M1 rifles to arm all its troops. It also remained in service as a sniper rifle during World War II, the Korean War, and even in the early stages of the Vietnam War.

The weapons used in the Mexican Revolution were as much the products of the Second Industrial Revolution and the turn-of-the-century arms race as they were of those used in other armed conflicts. Pancho Villa's forces in Mexico seem to have carried several different rifles during his career. The revolutionary troops were armed with Winchester M1895 (7.62mm) lever-action rifles and the Springfield M1903 bolt-action rifles. The famous shot with his sombrero'd and bandolier-festooned crew from early in the Revolution shows Villa with a 1910 Mauser carbine. These carbines were ubiquitous in the Revolution and were short enough to be handy from horseback, a definite asset for Villa's cavalry strike force. The rifles used by the Federales were the Mexican-made 7.7mm Mondragon rifle, which was the only semi-automatic rifle used in the revolution, and the German 7mm Mauser carbine and rifle. The Mondragon M1908 was Mexico's first self-loading rifle, and also one of the first such designs to see use in combat. The rifle had a characteristic inability to cope with ammunition of poor quality, however. This armed conflict is often categorized as the most important sociopolitical event in Mexico and one of the greatest upheavals of the 20th century.

Shotguns

The real coming of age for shotguns came in the 1880s, when gun makers introduced pump-action models that largely replaced the double barrel scattergun for military and agency use. A coach gun was a double-barreled shotgun, generally with two side-by-side barrels of about 18 inches in length. The name comes from the use of such shotguns on stagecoaches by shotgun messengers in the American Wild West. They often came in 10 gauge utilizing black powder. This class of shotguns was offered in a variety of barrel lengths from 12 to 20 inches either by the factory or from owners and gunsmiths cutting down the original barrels. These shotguns usually featured external hammers. A shotshell containing up to a dozen buckshot balls each of approximately .32 inches diameter was a devastator at short range. This was a very effective weapon when used against pursuing riders especially from a moving platform like a fleeing coach. The term *"Coach gun"* was coined in 1858 when Wells, Fargo & Co. began regular stagecoach service from Tipton, Missouri to San Francisco, California. They issued shotguns to their drivers and guards for defense along the perilous 2,800-mile route.

Like "gunslinger," the actual term "riding shotgun" first appeared in fiction about the Old West, dating back as far as 1905. It was later used in print and especially film depictions of stagecoaches and wagons in the Old West in danger of being robbed or attacked by bandits or Indians. In the 1939 classic film *Stagecoach*, actor George Bancroft plays Marshal Curly Wilcox who is featured *riding shotgun* in scenes throughout the film. The 1950s saw a spate of TV cowboy series in which *riding shotgun* was so commonplace in the scripts as to be almost obligatory. To date no researcher has found a citation for "riding shotgun" during the time in which stagecoaches were actually used.

A pump-action whether in a rifle or shotgun is one in which the handgrip can be pumped back and forth in order to eject a spent round of ammunition and to chamber a fresh one. It is much faster than a bolt-action and somewhat faster than a lever-action, as it does not require the trigger hand to be removed from the trigger while reloading. The weapon had a single barrel above a tube fed magazine into which additional shells were inserted. The cycling time of a pump-action is quite short. Older pump-action shotguns were often faster than modern semi-automatic shotguns, as they often did not have a trigger disconnect, and were capable of firing a new round as fast as the pump action was cycled, with the trigger held down continuously. This technique is called a slamfire.

The first pump action patent was issued to Alexander Bain of Britain in 1854. However, the Winchester Model 1893 was the first successful pump-action shotgun design to gain a commercial market share. A tougher, stronger and more improved version of the Winchester 1893, the Model 1897 was identical to its forerunner, except that the receiver was thicker and allowed for use of smokeless powder shells, which were not common at the time. The Model 1897 was popular before World War I, but it was after the war broke out that sales of the Model 1897 picked up. This was because many were produced to meet the trench warfare demands of the military. This model was ideal for close combat. Other military uses of the shotgun included guard and security operations, raids, ambushes, and encounters in urban environments. Messengers of The American Express Company were armed with this weapon, as were various police departments throughout the US.

Common US shotgun gauges are 10-, 12-, 16-, and 20-gauge with the 12- and 20-gauges being the most popular. The latter reflect the common calibers of hunting and military muskets used in the previous century. Samuel and Jacob Hawken claimed that the "plains rifle" produced by their shop was what their customers needed in the west, a quality gun, light enough to carry all the time, yet capable of knocking down big targets at long range. Their St. Louis, Missouri shop ran from 1815 to 1858. The rifles are generally shorter and of a larger caliber than earlier "Kentucky rifles" from which they descended. The half stock style of the rifles was the same as the Harpers Ferry Model 1803. The Hawken's "Rocky Mountain" guns were typically .50 caliber or .53 caliber, but ranged as high as .68 caliber. Meanwhile, the 24-gauge (0.580-inch) was the standard caliber (.580 and .577 caliber conical hollow base Minié balls) for Civil War rifled muskets. Once again, the common Enfield (.577) and Springfield (.580) weapons could tolerate either round, but the former was found to be more accurate, possibly because the British Enfield was better made.

Gauge	Caliber	Millimeter
4-gauge	0.935-inch	23.79mm
8-gauge	0.835-inch	21.21mm
10-gauge	0.775-inch	19.69mm
12-gauge	0.729-inch	18.53mm
14-gauge	0.693-inch	17.60mm
16-gauge	0.662-inch	16.83mm
20-gauge	0.615-inch	16.53mm
24-gauge	0.580-inch	14.73mm
28-gauge	0.550-inch	13.97mm
32-gauge	0.526-inch	13.36mm

The 4-, 8-, 14-, 24-, 28-, and 32-gauge were popular in the US and Europe to varying degrees in the past, but are virtually unheard of today, becoming the so-called "lost gauges." Both 14- and 28-gauge shotguns were widely used in the Old West along with the more common US gauges mentioned earlier. Unrealized by many, in the Old West the 10-gauge shotgun was very widely used. Doc Holiday of O.K. Corral gunfight fame carried a sawed off Belgium-made Meteor 10-gauge—termed the "street howitzer." Many 8-gauge shotguns saw popularity also. Shotguns larger than 10-gauge have been outlawed for hunting in the US since 1918.

Great care must be used to load the correct shell size into a shotgun in order to provide a proper gas seal on the breech end. Also a 20-gauge shell loaded into a 12-gauge shotgun may slip forward and catch on the front lip of the chamber, the chamber being slightly larger in diameter than the bore. When a break-open breech-loading shotgun is opened the chamber appears empty but the back of the shell is some inches down the chamber. A 12-gauge shell can inadvertently be loaded atop the 20-gauge. The explosive carnage thereafter can well be imagined. The 12-gauge 2-3/4-inch (70mm) long shell is standard in the US. The 3-inch (76mm) is a magnum load and it should never be attempted to load them into a 2-3/4-inch chamber. Most modern 12-gauge shotguns have 3-inch long chambers.

Centerfire and pinfire .410 shot cartridges first appeared in Eley Brothers Ltd. advertising flysheets in 1857. While not a standard "gauge," the .410 was quite popular because it had similar base dimensions to the .45 Colt revolver cartridge. By 1874 catalogs were advertising modern centerfire .410 cartridges. The fact that the .410 bore shell fits in a .45 Colt chamber has resulted in some unusual applications. various derringer models chambered both .45 Colt cartridges and .410 shotshell. It appears to have become popular around 1900, although it was recommended as "suited to the requirements of naturalists, and for such weapons as walking-stick guns," presumably for self-defense as early as 1892.[31]

5. On Offense and Defense

*All of our arms and ammunitions are experiments, and all our
theories of modern war, by sea or land, are empirical.*
—Stanhope Sams, *New York Times*, 16 August 1898

Pistols and Revolvers

When most people form a mental image of an Old West gun, however, they still see a revolver. After the Civil War, the Colt Peacemaker, more properly known as the Colt Model 1873, became the symbol of frontier life, westward expansion, and outlaw justice. It didn't take long for competitors to enter the market. Millions of guns like these—simple, rugged, easy-to-use weapons—have been used by pioneers, gunslingers, soldiers, police officers, homeowners and, of course, bad guys. Revolvers soon became standard for nearly all uses as handguns. Although they functioned admirably, military personnel, lawmen, and gun enthusiasts wanted more. In particular, they wanted two things revolvers had not yet delivered—faster reloading and greater capacity.[32]

Most modern revolvers are "traditional double-action," in that they may operate either in single-action or double-action mode. These designs were a culmination of many of the advances introduced in earlier weapons. In the late 19th century, semi-automatic pistols were developed, which could hold more rounds, and were faster to reload than most "wheel guns." While many western enthusiasts tend to think of semi-automatic pistols as more modern, it should be remembered that by the turn of the century the introduction of the venerable and widely imitated Colt Model 1911 was a little more than a decade away, and small-caliber semi-autos were already in wide use. The low pressures produced by many pistol cartridges at the time simplified their development. There are numerous cases of early 20th century lawmen carrying not only traditional single-actions but also new Colt and S&W double actions in .38 caliber, Colt's .38 ACP Models 1900-1903 semi-autos, as well as imported guns like the FN Browning 1900, C96 Mauser, and 9 mm Luger Parabellum.

In the US the traditional single-action revolver still reigned supreme until the late 19th century, but European arms makers were quick to adopt the double-action trigger. While the US was producing powerful single-action weapons like the Colt Army or S&W Schofield, the Europeans were building somewhat less powerful double-action models like the French MAS Modèle 1873 and the somewhat later British Enfield Mk I and II revolvers. The velocity and power of the MAS, in variants equivalent to the .25 and .32 calibers, was weak for its time, while the top-break British Enfield came in as a surprisingly robust .455 caliber at the relatively low velocity of 650 fps. Nonetheless, the latter cartridge was rated superior to the .45 Colt in stopping power in the disputed United States Thompson-LaGarde Tests of 1904. The results are contested to this day as having been unscientific.

Colt's first attempt at a double action revolver to compete with the European manufacturers was the Colt Model 1877, a design widely considered to be overly complicated. The need for simplicity of repair in the expanses of the Old West may have added to the reputation and lasting popularity of the single-action revolver. In 1889, Colt introduced the Model 1889, the first truly modern double-action revolver, which differed from earlier double action revolvers by having a "swing-out" cylinder, as opposed to a "top-break" or "side-loading" cylinder. Swing out cylinders quickly caught on, because they combined the best reloading features of earlier designs. The Colt Model 10 of 1899 went on to become the best selling handgun of the 20th century at 6 million units. Revolvers have remained popular to the present day although in the military and in law enforcement, magazine-fed semi-automatic pistols have largely supplanted them.

Knock Down Power

The concept of knock down power, or stopping power was not formalized during the Old West period. It probably existed as an anecdotal impression among firearms experts and hunters. Rather predictably, professional hunters on the Old West prairies found that some buffalo dropped where they were shot and some didn't, even though all received near-identical hits in the vital heart-lung area. Some calibers seemed to just flatten the game while others were not as dependable. Anecdotal information from the Crimean War and American Civil War favored large calibers, but the more formalized idea of stopping power surfaced in the late 19th Century when European and American colonial troops fighting at close quarters with supposed "technologically inferior" opponents found that their pistols were not able to stop charging native tribesmen, notably Chinese Boxers (1899-1901) and Moros (1901-1913) for Americans. The concept of knockdown power does not seem to have been a consideration among US forces in their wars with Native Americans largely because it had not yet surfaced as a well-formulated idea. Although higher caliber has traditionally been widely associated with higher stopping power, the physics involved are multifactorial, with caliber, muzzle velocity, bullet mass, bullet shape, bullet material, and shooter skill in the placement of shots all contributing to the mix. [33]

It is also known that Native American warriors avoided attacking buffalo hunters because they feared the gruesome power, long range, and reloading speed of the Sharps falling block .52 buffalo rifles and their 475 grain bullets. The Sharps, which fired a solid bullet at up to 1300 fps, was often used to fight Indians because it could knock down a Native's horse at a hundred yards or more. The carbine version was notable in the Civil War. It was a popular hunting rifle that led to the introduction of several derivatives in quick succession. It handled a large number of .40- to .50-caliber cartridges in a variety of loadings and barrel lengths.

At the Second Battle of Adobe Wells (1874), for instance, the Comanche and Kiowa were well armed, but their lever action rifles were chambered in .44 rimfire or .44-40 — short-range pistol caliber weapons. Losing the element of surprise, the warriors started taking casualties from the fire of the heavy rifles of the buffalo hunters who were well protected in a sod brick store-saloon. An Army Scout among the hunters, William "Billy" Dixon, already renowned as a crack shot, took aim with a "Big Fifty" Sharps (it was either a .50-70 or .50-90 cartridge conversion), and cleanly dropped a warrior from atop his horse from almost a mile away (1500 yards). Dixon went into the history books for firing "*The Shot of the Century*" which effectively ended the siege.

Buffalo Stand

In 1870, a new technique for tanning buffalo hides became commercially available, and commercial hunters began systematically targeting buffalo for the first time. The destruction of the buffalo herds was a disaster for the Plains Indians, on and off the reservations. Generally, they resisted the destruction of their traditional way of life. Up to twenty separate engagements between soldiers and Native Americans may have taken place in the Texas Panhandle alone. Archeological evidence gathered from the battle sites of the Red River War (1874) indicates that the Indians were primarily using repeating rifles such as the Spencer that fired a .50 caliber cartridge and could fire seven rounds before reloading, and the Winchester or Henry rifles that fired a 200 grain .44 caliber bullet backed by 25 grains of black powder. Each could hold up to 15 rounds of ammunition, but their effective range was less than 200 yards.

Sharps made sporting versions of its military weapons from the late 1840s until the late 1880s.

There is no question that market forces nearly marked the bison for extinction sooner than had buffalo been left to the Indians alone. Four hundred yards downwind from a grazing herd of buffalo, a hunter rests the barrel of his .50 caliber Sharps on a metal monopod, cocks the hammer and sights in on a victim. Hit in the lungs, the animal remains stationary while its lifeblood flows from the wound, and it calmly collapses. Not realizing that one of their number has been mortally wounded, the other members of the herd continue grazing. Within minutes the process is repeated. The shots from the discharge of a black powder Sharps rifle resembled thunder, a familiar sound to buffalo living on the plains. Such is the myth of the Buffalo Stand.

For the buffalo hunter of the 1870s and 1880s, shot placement was important if he hoped to have more than one kill. Buffalo hunters occasionally did shoot every animal in a small herd, but the buffalo were not unmindful of the carnage. According to R.G. Robertson of *True West Magazine* (1 July 2002), buffalo would not tolerate such a wounded animal in their midst. As soon as the first buffalo in a herd was shot, the smell of blood would send the rest of the herd into a frenzy—circling and hooking, and attempting to draw in outlying members of the herd for protection. This behavior has been observed many times.

Another myth to be exploded is that of the Native American living in harmony with nature while greedy Europeans raped the continent. Instead, evidence suggests that

Indians employed communal strategies on a large-scale burning to "clear" forests and also to kill game. The controlled burns employed by the Indians often flashed through the forests or over the grasslands, destroying everything in their path. Many species were already on a trajectory to extinction in some areas, because over and above the hunting done by Indians, natural predators, and disasters thinned the herds. The North American bison herd may already have been falling below replacement levels before white hunters arrived. Estimates made in the 1850s suggest that Indians harvested about 450,000 animals a year, and some think the figure was far higher. Westward expansion of whites and trade between whites and Indians produced two significant changes, one more destructive than the other. The first was that many Indians shifted from a farming to a nomadic, hunting lifestyle. The second was that the Natives acquired a combination of horses and firearms that made their hunting terribly efficient. [34]

Most likely, the Indians acquired the Spencers, Winchesters, and Henrys after the Civil War when large numbers of these weapons became available to frontier traders and gunrunners. With the Indians using repeating rifles and the Army using single shot weapons, it might appear that the Indians had the superior arms. In fact, many officers who served the Union during the Civil War and were familiar with the Spencer's firepower were very reluctant to exchange the repeating Spencer for the new single shot Springfield .45-70 carbine. However, many other officers came to believe that the single shot Springfield was a superior weapon to the Spencer. The new .45-70 caliber Springfield cartridge had greater accuracy and velocity at longer ranges.

Lethality

A bullet potentially has high lethality if it does great damage to the flesh of a living body. Extremely high projectile speed can result in high lethality. Without such speed, large projectile diameter and weight (mass) can also result in high lethality. A bullet with a relatively small cross-sectional area and with what sounds like a small amount of kinetic energy behind it, can deliver considerable energy per square inch when making contact. A modern energy measurement of 85 Joules (63 ft-lbs) is often cited as NATO's minimum cutoff for lethality. Very few rounds (outside those designed strictly for target shooting and plinking) are designed to produce less than this minimum. For comparison, a professional baseball pitch throws a fastball with about 2 joules (1.5 ft-lbs) of energy.

Some very popular myths, misconceptions, and miscalculations concerning the terminal effects of bullets are strongly held, and it is not the purpose of this discussion to demonstrate why they are or are not true. There are always anecdotal accounts that can be found of people being hurled off their feet by a .45 when a pathetic little .38 is being shrugged off without effect. In actuality, there are quite as many incidents of people shrugging off .45 slugs as for many lesser calibers. When gun writers attempt to describe terminal ballistics in terms more technical than "wallop," they bear the responsibility to convey an accurate discussion of the mechanisms involved.

There is a prevalent belief that a bullet, which remains inside a target, is more effective in terms of stopping or killing power than one which completely penetrates or over-penetrates. The idea seems to be that all of the kinetic energy has been spent inside the game animal or opponent. It is interesting that the 19th century model of "energy dump" required the bullet to completely pass through the body, but stop under the skin on the off-side. The "penetration" school of thought affords the depth of the wound channel considerable value, while the "cavitation" experts give greater weight to the shape of the wound channel internally. The critical issue here is what sort of hole was made, not whether it goes all the way through. The human frame is so lightly constructed that any "stopper" class weapon will easily penetrate through even after encountering major bones.

Tragically, Americans seems to place about as much confidence in the science of numbers as in superstition. Bigger is always considered better. There is a prevalent and unscientific tendency to believe that lethality is attributable to the cartridge chambering, rather than to the bullet mass and impact velocity. Applying this myth in isolation the .75 caliber Brown Bess musket would be more lethal than any number of .30 caliber weapons from WWII.

The .22 LR was regarded as a "whimpy" round, but it appeared in a large number of firearms that were designed around it nonetheless. The small size of the round allowed a large number to be carried with ease or to be chambered in large numbers. Eight, nine, and ten cartridge cylinders were very important when reloading was a laborious and time-consuming task. US Fire Arms of Hartford actually produced a twelve-chambered .22 LR revolver.

Because a .22 LR bullet is less powerful than larger cartridges, its danger to humans is often underestimated, but well placed it can be lethal. The type originated from the Flobert BB cap of 1845 through the .22 Smith & Wesson cartridge of 1857. For many decades, it has been a very popular cartridge around the world. It is one of the few cartridges that are accepted by such a large variety of rifles and pistols. As a hunting cartridge, .22 LR rimfires are mainly used to kill small game. Performance varied with barrel length and the type of action. For example, bolt-action rifles may perform differently from semiautomatic rifles and pistols from revolvers. Generally, a longer barrel with no blowback will produce a more energetic bullet at the muzzle.

Doing Damage

The primary objective of most Old West gunfights was to put the other guy out of the fight, not necessarily to kill him. Of course, a dead opponent no longer posed a threat. Yet it was altogether possible that both participants of an encounter might die—one immediately or soon thereafter, and the wounded winner some time later after a long period of incapacity, infection, and illness. The idea was not to be hit in the first place.

Bullets can also cause disabling injuries other than death that prevent specific actions. Bullets that strike a major bone (such as a femur) can expend their entire energy into the surrounding tissue, causing it to take on a gelled consistency as the cellular structure is destroyed. The struck bone is commonly shattered at the point of impact and made incapable of supporting the body. A broken arm, shattered shoulder or hip can also incapacitate.

Some firearms experts choose to measure bullet momentum rather than bullet energy when making comparisons. This is unfortunate. Momentum is an intellectual construct that helps physicists understand the interaction of pieces of matter, but it does not exist as a real entity. It has more to do with recoil than external ballistics. (OK! I've been teaching physics for more than four decades.) Moreover, momentum is the result of the mathematical differentiation of energy in any case. Energy is real! It does the damage. The calculation of momentum does not properly describe the effect of added velocity to the equation—incorrectly ascribing to *added mass* the same effect as *added velocity*. In reality, adding velocity to a bullet increases its energy in proportion to the square of the increase. In other words, the same bullet moving twice as fast has four times the energy, three times as fast, nine times the energy, and so on. A bullet moving just 10 percent faster (880 fps v 800 fps) has a 21 percent increase in energy, but only a 10 percent increase in momentum.

Effective Range

The United States Army used many guns in the Indian Wars. The six shot .45 caliber Colt single action revolver was the service pistol of choice in 1874. The effective range of the Colt revolver dropped off rapidly over 60 yards, but it was a killer within this limited range. In the 1870s, the Army mostly used the repeating Spencer carbine, the Sharps cartridge carbine, and the Springfield single shot .50-caliber rifle as long arms. The Springfield was effective at 400 yards with a velocity of almost 1200 fps. Its maximum range was about 1000 yards. The infantry began to use the .45 Trapdoor Springfield (45-70) in 1873 and the cavalry used the same caliber, but with a shorter barrel. The model 1866 trapdoor had seen limited issue to troops along the Bozeman Trail in 1867. These .45 and .50 calibers rifles were single shot. The black powder model 1873 continued to be the main service rifle of the U.S. Military until it was gradually replaced by the Springfield model 1892 bolt-action rifle.

In 1872–1873 a military board, headed by Brigadier-General Alfred H. Terry, conducted an examination and trial of 99 rifles from several domestic and foreign manufacturers including those from Springfield, Sharps, Peabody, Whitney, Spencer, Remington, and Winchester pursuant to the selection of a breech-loading system for rifles and carbines for the US military. The trials included tests for: accuracy, dependability, rate-of-fire, and ability to withstand adverse conditions. Both single shot and magazine equipped systems were considered but, at the time, the single shot was deemed to be more reliable. The Army decision makers generally avoided the adoption of magazine fed weapons because they feared that the soldiers would fire rounds promiscuously and stress the logistics of their supply trains.

Effective range for a firearm is not typically considered a one-time determination. This is the maximum range at which an average shooter can hit a human-sized target 50 percent of the time. After traversing 1000 yards (3000 feet) most 19th century bullets were no longer considered lethal. A so-called "spent bullet" if fired at an arc to achieve its maximum range will cause little to no actual damage, usually a big bruise. This was a common occurrence in the Civil War where riflemen were attempting hits at what were novel maximum ranges. Gettysburg hero of Little Round Top in 1863, Joshua Lawrence Chamberlain sustained two slight wounds in the battle, one when a shot hit his sword scabbard and bruised his thigh, and another when a spent bullet or piece of shrapnel hit his right foot. Nonetheless, at Spotsylvania Court House Federal General John Sedgwick was killed by a sniper shooting from 800 yards. Famously, Sedgwick had recently admonished his own men concerning their fear of snipers: "I am ashamed of you! They couldn't hit an elephant at this distance!"

It is remarkable that no outstanding modern studies are ongoing in this area, but there are so many confounding factors that the conclusions might be ambiguous in any case. Nineteenth century weapons expert Julian Hatcher actually tested five hundred rounds of .30-06 150-grain bullets for terminal energy by shooting them straight up in the air and then observing how they penetrated a board when they fell to the ground. It was concluded from these tests that the return velocity was about 300 fps. With the 150-grain bullet this corresponds to an energy of 30 ft-lbs. Previously the Army had decided that on the average, an energy of 60 ft-lbs was required to produce a disabling wound. Nonetheless, bullets traveling at just 250 fps will penetrate skin 50 percent of the time. Thus service bullets returning from extreme heights cannot be considered lethal by this standard. This does not mean that they are not dangerous. Take as an analogy in this regard a bullet dropped from the top of a skyscraper. Its kinetic energy is considerable enough to be avoided, but hardly ballistic in nature.

A bullet fired from a weapon on an angle with the ground never completely stops in such a fashion, however, hitting with far greater speed and energy then reached in these terminal velocity studies. For example, a bullet fired at an angle of 30 degrees with the ground begins with 86.6 percent of its muzzle velocity in the horizontal direction but does not retain it all throughout its flight. Even at 45 degrees, which some will improperly consider the angle that will give the greatest range, the initial horizontal energy is almost 70.7 percent. Yet air resistance robs it of this energy both on the way up and on the way down. In fact, it is the factor of great distance that creates the "spent" bullet. Yet the Earth usually gets in the way long before air friction stops the horizontal motion of a bullet fired under the latter specified conditions. The trajectory of such projectiles is never a symmetrical parabola in any case. The "target" side of the path is much more pronounced toward the ground than the "shooter's" side, approaching straight down at extreme ranges. These factors make Hatcher's method of straight up and straight down both convenient and appropriate for his time and level of technology. [35]

Shooting up or down hill at a significant angle also has its effects. Firing up or down a significant slope–as at the Battle of Missionary Ridge where it was found that the majority of shot from both attackers and defenders went into the treetops–produced a profound distortion in the line-of-sight path of a bullet if steps were not taken to correct for the effects of gravity especially at long ranges. Most Civil War soldiers did not spend their time in such analyses. On the defensive "the vast majority of soldiers in the Union and Confederate armies received no training in estimating distances and therefore were not prepared to effectively fire their muskets at long-range targets." Officers and NCOs constantly admonished the men under their command to "aim low" in order to offset this characteristic of Civil War musket fire. Moreover, without the aid of optical devices like telescopic sights, it was difficult to identify specific targets at extreme ranges leaving soldiers the option of withholding their fire until the enemy approached or indiscriminately lobbing bullets into a distant mass of enemy troops in the hope of hitting something. "Civil War commanders and soldiers alike preferred to wait until the enemy came quite close before opening fire," a distance (between 100 and 120 yards) found by battlefield researchers to be quite consistent with the range (if not the poor accuracy) of smoothbore muskets from the previous century. [36]

Everything that affects a projectile from launch through flight to impact will influence the injuries it can cause. Also, where on the body the projectile strikes makes a tremendous difference in the injury caused and its prognosis. Temporary cavity formation is a significant component of the resulting injury from a bullet, and that is influenced by the energy of the projectile at impact, whether it was flying straight and steadily or wobbling and tumbling. The physiological state of the person who has been shot can make a difference, as well. Some people can be shot only once in the chest by a small handgun before they fall to the ground and cease to be a threat. However, police reports have numerous stories of officers unloading six rounds from their standard-issue handgun directly into the chest of an assailant only to be attacked and hurt by them.

Service and Agency Weapons

Of the many debatable topics of conversation in the firearms world, one that pops up a lot more often than others relates to caliber. The design for the turn of the century Army service handgun was created around a 38 caliber bullet—essentially a modern 9 mm or .380 (9 mm short) both of which are popular today. The .38 Special with a 158 grain bullet was introduced in 1898 as an improvement over the .38 Long Colt, and served as a standard for many police agencies and the FBI for decades. Alternatively, the famed M1911 .45 ACP seems to have won the battle as a service weapon for the military up to 1985.

The fact is that modern armies have learned that they don't need or want weapons that kill enemy soldiers. On the battlefield just putting enemy soldiers out of the fight has added benefits. The enemy must use resources to carry away and treat injured comrades, and friendly soldiers can carry more bullets to put more enemy soldiers out of commission since the bullets are smaller and lighter than more lethal bullets. Fifty rounds of 9 mm weigh approximately one pound less than an equal quantity of .45 ACP. Similarly, the objective of police and law enforcement is to eliminate the threat. When this objective can be accomplished without killing the target, so much the better. Each of these groups is mired in decades-old arguments.

Gen. John T. Thompson, a West Point graduate, was assigned to the Army's Ordnance Department in 1890, where he was to spend the bulk of his military career. During this period, he began his specialization in small arms. Until the outbreak of the Spanish-American War in 1898, Thompson's military service was routine and uneventful. During the War, he used his weapons training to its fullest advantage. He became a small arms specialist, and took charge of the Army's ordnance supplies and logistics during the invasion of Cuba. In 1904, Thompson and Col. Louis A. LaGarde of the Medical Corps conducted several tests designed to find the caliber most suited for military handgun ammunition.

It is interesting to observe that experts are still arguing this basic question of terminal ballistics, which was articulated by Thompson in 1904, several wars and more than 100 years ago! The wrestling match in the terminal ballistics field is currently between the "small and fast" corner, and the "big and slow" corner. This discussion quickly degenerates into a lot of arcane mumbles about temporary and permanent crush cavities, energy transfer, hydrostatic shock, and expansion coefficients. It's interesting if you're a physicist or a forensic pathologist, but it gets kind of academic for everyone else.

Unfortunately, other experts claim that the information that many agencies use to choose their munitions are often based on myth and anecdote as well as the flawed standardized testing and measurements of the depth of penetration, degree of bullet expansion, and other factors in so-called ballistic gel. Usually, actual data on human body wound ballistics is not available to agencies when they are choosing standard munitions. What is most unfortunate is that the testing of bullets does not give a complete picture of what a particular ammunition configuration will do in the human body to incapacitate it in a timely fashion, in other words, stopping power. The term stopping power has been a marketing tool since that time and should be dropped from discussions of ballistic performance until ammunition effectiveness can be measured by better means. [37]

During the same time frame that John Browning was working on many of his 128 firearms patents, a tribe of warriors known as the Moro was giving the US Army a very hard time in the Philippines. To prepare for battle, the Moro would bind their limbs with leather, take narcotics, and use painful religious rituals to gain an altered state of consciousness that seemingly turned them into virtual Supermen. In such a state, the warrior's mind would no longer register additional external pain. The .38 Long Colt revolver cartridge (the .38 referring to the approximate diameter of the loaded brass case rather than the bullet) that US soldiers had at the time simply would not stop the Moro unless it killed him outright. The Army Ordnance Board determined that the Army needed a .45 caliber cartridge to provide adequate stopping power. Browning therefore re-engineered a .38 autoloader that he had planned in order to accommodate a .45 diameter lead round nose bullet. The .45 (1225 fps and 600 ft-lbs) was more effective than the .38 as a pistol cartridge (777 fps and only 200 ft-lbs). Of note is the fact that the .30 caliber Krag rifles the US issued (more than 1900 fps and 1700 ft-lbs of energy depending on ammunition) were also seemingly useless against the Moro. The .45 ACP was not issued in the Philippines during the Moro uprising, but the experience with the Moros led the Army to specify the .45 for its new service autoloader.

Browning is most frequently remembered as the designer of the 1911 .45 ACP and the Browning High Power. The High Power name alludes to the 13-round 9 mm magazine capacity, almost twice that of contemporary designs such as the Colt M1911. Browning died in 1926, several years before the High Power design was finalized. He also created the Winchester .30-30, the Winchester Pump Shotgun, the Browning Auto-5 Shotgun (produced by Remington as the Model 11), the BAR (Browning .30 caliber Automatic Rifle) and the Browning .50 caliber Machine Gun, plus most of the .30 caliber and .50 caliber machine guns produced by Colt and used in WW II.

Browning began to experiment with self-loaders in 1889, inspired by Hiram S. Maxim who had invented a machine gun six years earlier. Browning converted a Winchester 1873 lever-action to an autoloader by using the action of the expanding gases at the muzzle. A machine gun using this same operating principle was built in 1890 and 1891. Browning's Model 1911 pistol was the first firearm to undergo such comprehensive testing, firing continuously 6000 cartridges, a record broken only in 1917 when Browning's recoil-operated machine gun fired a 40,000 rounds test. One hundred shots would be fired and the weapon would be allowed to cool for 5 minutes.

After World War I, the Army's Ordnance Department evaluated the Colt .45's combat performance as positive. The cartridge exhibited relatively low muzzle blast and flash, as well as moderate recoil. The Ordnance Board indicated that the pistol had functioned well in an operating environment characterized by high usage in training, rough handling and environments on deployments and limited access to repair and maintenance resources. "The Ordnance Board was of the opinion that a bullet, which will have the shock effect and stopping effect at short ranges necessary for a military pistol or revolver, should have a caliber not less than .45." But they also said that "soldiers armed with pistols or revolvers should be drilled unremittingly in the accuracy of fire" because most of the human body offered "no hope of stopping an adversary by shock or other immediate results when hit." [38]

The man who pushed the Army into adopting the .45 caliber cartridge was John T. Thompson, the father of the Thompson submachine gun (which also fired the .45 ACP) and a member of the Army Ordnance Board during the time that the M1911 pistol was being developed. Thompson was committed to the idea that the Army should be packing a real man-stopper in its handguns, a big .45 caliber bullet. It was the cartridge tested by Thompson and LaGarde in 1904 at the Nelson Morris Company Union Stockyards in Chicago where they tested various calibers on live cattle, deer, and human cadavers to determine the best load.

After its adoption in 1911, the .45 automatic cartridge was a playground for all possible tests, changes, types (blank, dummies, high pressure, tracer, high velocity, perforating, hollow, jacketed, sport, etc.) for military, police and civilian use. Today, a multitude of .45 auto cartridges exists. Even in its non-expanding full metal jacket (FMJ) version, the .45 ACP cartridge has a reputation for effectiveness against human targets because its large diameter creates a deep and substantial permanent wound channel which lowers blood pressure rapidly. The specifications of today's .45 auto cartridges are similar to the one finally adopted in 1911. They operate at a relatively low maximum chamber pressure rating of 21,000 psi (compared to 35,000 psi for 9mm Parabellum).

The 9mm is having something of a renaissance these days. Although maligned in the past due to its seeming inability to reliably deliver immediate incapacitating force, recent technological developments in bullet and propellant design have moved the round back to the forefront for many law enforcement departments, and it has been chosen as the standard caliber for US and NATO handguns.

Some reports suggest, however, that the US Marines are not happy with their main Beretta M9s for their lack of accuracy and stopping power. Even though Uncle Sam selected the higher-capacity M9, it was quite obvious that the Marines still wanted the power from the legendary .45. With M1911's continued to supply Special Ops and Recon needs, renewed interest in the M1911 as a better solution may again be growing (M45A1 Close Quarters Battle Pistol (CQBP)).

Yet it is safe to say that all pistol cartridges are inadequate in terms of real power when compared to modern hunting rifles. Handguns have their place due to the ease with which they can be carried and brought into action, but it's important to recognize that no fighting force in history has gone into battle armed with pistols as their primary weapons. The area in which a bullet will be lethal is very small, making repeated precise shot placement more important than bullet size. Unfortunately large caliber handguns tend to exhibit a good deal of recoil making precise second and third shots more difficult. (See *Gunfight Tactics* below)

Although it had finally showed signs of petering out, the "9mm versus .45 ACP" dispute, which sold so much ink for the gun press over the years, has risen once again. The FBI was initially unsatisfied with the performance of the 9 mm bullet. Yet these agencies have taken an honest look at the demographics of their personnel, and have accepted the fact that law enforcement officers of both genders often come with smaller hands and shorter fingers that find it difficult to reach the controls on larger caliber pistols with their corresponding larger frames. A smaller-frame pistol in a milder shooting caliber allows more officers to achieve the control necessary for good shooting, and makes sense for diverse agencies that want to standardize on a single gun and caliber. True professionals will let the amateurs bicker about minute differences in equipment.

6. By the Numbers

Lethality

Given a projectile's speed, diameter and weight, the lethality can be increased by doing things that cause the bullet cross-section to increase in area as it goes through the body. For example, this is done by making modern projectiles with a soft nose or with devices such as hollow points or Teflon coated wedges. The equivalent kinetic energy of a typical .45 ACP 200 grain bullet is that of a 60 pound weight (three and a half bowling balls) dropped from a height of 10 feet as compared to that of the .38 Long Colt revolver cartridge with a 158 grain bullet, a 20 pound weight (about one bowling ball) dropped from the same height. Both situations are probably lethal if precisely aimed. The only other handgun cartridge, which has demonstrated stopping power comparable to the .45 ACP is the 125 grain .357 Magnum jacketed hollow point designed in 1934.

Lacking both high speed and physical embellishments, increasing the weight of the bullet seemed a reasonable alternative for 19th century shooters. What emerges from this discussion is that nearly all big game cartridges are capable of killing essentially any size game animal (or human) under ideal conditions even with a single, solid, spherical lead bullet. Yet well-placed small caliber bullets can also be lethal. [39]

General Julian Hatcher, a noted forensic pathologist and firearms expert, in the early 1920s developed a formulation to determine the theoretical stopping power of a firearm cartridge. His formula has withstood the test of time and validation from other studies and data related to stopping power. A Hatcher rating of a handgun cartridge under 30 only has about a 30% chance of producing a one shot stop. Hatcher ratings of 30 to 49 raise a one shot stop to approximately a 50% chance. Ratings of 50 or higher produce a one shot stop about 90% of the time. The .45 ACP round nose lead projectile has a rating of 49.1 while its hollow point cousin of the same 200 grains is a 60.7. Yet this is not the end of the story. The early hollow points did not feed reliably through the M1911 government automatic pistol while the solid lead bullets rarely failed to feed. Some of the older 1911 pistols don't like hollow point bullets even today and have to be throated and have their feed ramps polished for reliability. Meanwhile the reliable .38 Special revolver cartridge is rated at 39.7 from a three-inch barrel and slightly higher as the barrel length increases. Today the 9 mm round (essentially a .380) has been adopted in order to align with the cartridges used by most foreign and NATO agencies. The 9 mm has a bullet mass of just 124 grains as compared to the .45 at 200+ grains. Hatcher did his studies between the World Wars. He was Chief of Field Service, Ordnance Department, during the most critical years of World War II. His many comprehensive books and informative publications on firearms were widely used by both military and civilian agencies, particularly the Federal Bureau of Investigation.[40]

These developments also have a more troubling human history with their folio of potential discrepancies. The weapon used to kill Abraham Lincoln in 1865 was an essentially obsolete single shot .41 Derringer muzzleloader fired with a percussion cap from no more than a few inches away at 400 fps, but the gun used to kill James Garfield in 1881 was a Belgian-made British Bulldog black powder revolver in .44 short centerfire. Both weapons fired a generally large bullet. At twenty feet, the first shot missed Garfield but the second fatally wounded the latter President. British Bulldog revolvers of a similar type using smokeless powder were popular into the 20th century. It took two shots from a smaller centerfire .32-caliber Iver-Johnson revolver to fatally wound William McKinley in 1901.

Garfield survived eleven weeks after being shot, a long time compared with the other presidents who were assassinated: Lincoln died nine hours after being shot, McKinley survived for a week before dying. In 1963, John F. Kennedy died almost instantly being hit in the head with a 6.5 mm jacketed rifle cartridge (U.S. version: .25 Winchester at 2500 fps) at a distance of more than 80 yards and a depressed angle of aim of 17 degrees. It should be remembered that the blame for the *misuse* of a firearm is to be placed on the shooter, not the firearm, its developer, or its manufacturer.

On October 14, 1912, an unemployed saloonkeeper shot former president and Progressive Party candidate Theodore Roosevelt outside a Milwaukee hotel. The .38 caliber bullet from a Colt revolver 5 feet away was slowed by a written 50-page speech that Roosevelt planned to give folded double in his breast pocket. Although there were no outward signs of blood, the former president reached inside his heavy overcoat and felt a dime-sized bullet hole on the right side of his chest. Having handled guns as a hunter, a cowboy, and an officer during the Spanish-American War, Roosevelt knew enough to put a finger to his lips to see if he was bleeding from the mouth. When he saw that he was not, he concluded that the bullet had not entered his lung. "He pinked me," Roosevelt told a party official, but he made the speech. After a few words, the former "Rough Rider" pulled the torn and bloodstained manuscript from his breast pocket and declared, "You see, it takes more than one bullet to kill a Bull Moose." He spoke for nearly 90 minutes and then was rushed to the hospital. Doctors determined it was safer to leave the bullet embedded deep in Roosevelt's chest than to operate. Ironically, Roosevelt carried a gun of similar caliber and make during the Spanish-American War and for his personal self-defense. Roosevelt's frank statements to his intimates that he believed in being prepared for emergencies, showed that he fully realized the danger to which a public man of his prominence was exposed, particularly at times of popular excitement when cranks and anarchists were likely to seek notoriety by attempting assassinations. [41]

In 1981, President Ronald Reagan was shot in the chest, below the left underarm. He suffered a punctured lung and heavy internal bleeding, but prompt medical attention allowed him to recover quickly. The would-be assassin fired a modern .22 caliber revolver six times missing the president with all but one shot, but wounding three others. The bullet used was a Devastator Hollow Point (a lacquer sealed aluminum tip with a lead azide center designed to explode on impact). Whether Devastator bullets actually explode or cause greater damage than "non-exploding" bullets is a matter of debate among experts, but they agree that such bullets most often fail to work as designed.

The Devastator bullet was developed in the 1970s for use by sky marshals, to minimize the risk of penetration of the plane fuselage when incapacitating a hijacker. The bullet was voluntarily removed from the market in 1994, but is available to law enforcement. Despite anti-gun media assertions, these projectiles are not armor piercing nor a means to overcome ballistic vests. True exploding bullets were first described over a century ago and, although not actually in use at that time, were prohibited under the St Petersburg Declaration of 1868, which states that explosive or inflammable projectiles, with a weight of less than 400 g, should never be used in the time of war. The exception was made for the explosive shells of light artillery.

The concept of using a hollow point (HP) to enhance a rifle bullet's terminal performance came about in the late 1880s. Interestingly, the primary motivation behind the HP design was to reduce the bullet's weight, and hence increase its velocity, without changing the bullet's length, thereby allowing the same rifling pitch to be used. These bullets were also found to perform exceptionally well from revolvers.

The last decades of the 19th century were the golden age of Express Loads: lighter bullets driven to the highest velocities attainable with black powder. All of these bullets performed best when cast fairly soft, typically about 20-to-1 lead to tin for standard velocities. This marriage of bullet design and lead alloys was truly exceptional. These HP bullets were promoted as hunting rounds being able to "increase the killing power of these rifles by 50%." However, due to the common practice of the day to chamber both revolvers and lever-guns in the same cartridges for frontier expediency, it became possible to load and shoot cast HP ammo in revolvers as well. As a result, cast HPs made their handgun debut in Old West six guns chambered for a number of common calibers.[42]

Tactical considerations concerning bullet penetration are a different matter entirely. The minimum lethal wound surface area for ideal performance by a projectile can be estimated. A well-placed arrow strike can be as lethal as that of a massive bullet. (See: Jan Friis-Hansen) In practice, a bullet will require a somewhat larger area to offset the crushing mechanism of cavitation that promotes coagulation of the blood. The single most important factor in wound lethality is projectile placement in either case. This cannot be overstated. It is worth remembering that the majority of authorities agree that recoil of over twenty foot pounds will cause most shooters to develop a serous flinch, which is ruinous to bullet placement.

Direct hits against the base of the brain (as with JFK) or the upper spine are almost always instantly fatal because these regions control the involuntary vital functions like heartbeat and respiration. When Dr. Charles Leale, the first physician to arrive, gained entrance into the Lincoln theater box, the President was visibly dead. He had no respiratory rate. He had no pulse. The initial track of the bullet and the cavity being instantaneously formed and then collapsing back in on itself caused the damage. The ball seemingly hemorrhaged the brain and lodged behind the eye. Lincoln didn't bleed to death; he died because of the swelling that caused the brain stem to herniate down the spinal canal opening at the base of his skull. Although Lincoln's respiration was reinstituted, brain death was assured. In the case of hemorrhage resulting from damage to the lungs or arteries, brain death will also likely occur prior to cessation of cardiac function.[43]

Victims of wounds to the body in gunfights often fell down instantly, seemingly dead, only to rise up an instant later as the initial shock of the wounding passed. This fascinating observation supported the existence of an incapacitating mechanism known as temporary neurological paralysis. The phenomenon from which this misunderstanding arises is simply trauma to the central nervous system. It is equally possible under these circumstances for the release of adrenaline from the wounding to redouble the activity of the target. Critics contend that the importance of a "one-shot stop" is overstated, pointing out that most gun encounters do not involve a shoot once and see how the target reacts scenario. In a combat scenario, most shooters fire until the enemy goes down. Even with large calibers, a second or third shot commonly follows. In a word, the inherent stopping power of a single bullet is a *myth*. [44]

A double tap is a shooting technique where two shots are fired in rapid succession at the same target with the same sight picture. British police chiefs working in Shanghai during the 1930s developed the technique in order to overcome the expansion limitations of full metal jacket (FMJ) ammunition. The so-called Mozambique Drill developed in the mid-20th century (1964-1974) is intended to ensure that a human opponent is immediately stopped, by first placing two shots into the larger, easier-to-hit mass of the upper body (called a double tap maneuver); then, if the target is still active, following with a third, more precisely aimed head or spine shot. These tactics are still used today by firearms handlers, police tactical teams, military personnel, counter-terrorist combat units, and other Special Operations Forces personnel.

Historically, only one type of ammunition has had the specific trade name "Manstopper." Officially known as the Mk III cartridge, these were made to suit the British Webley .455 service revolver in the early 20th century. The ammunition used a 220-grain cylindrical bullet with hemispherical depressions at both ends. The front acted as a hollow point deforming on impact while the base opened to seal the round in the barrel. It was introduced in 1898, but removed from service in 1900 as it raised concerns at the Hague Convention.

Going Automatic

Quick, multiple shots were very difficult to deliver with single action handguns. Double action relieved the situation somewhat, but shooters expressed a desire for more robust defensive systems. Successful self-loading handguns began appearing in the 1890s. The United States Army evaluated several semi-automatic pistols in the late 19th century.

One operating issue with all early light blowback pistols, however, was that the slide might not cycle properly if the pistol was fired with a weak grip in the firing hand. Unlike the more reliable revolvers, in these small automatics a firm grip and a hefty hand was often required for their proper operation. The tremendous recoil of larger caliber weapons such as the .45 ACP or 9 mm largely obviated this factor.

Joseph Laumann produced the first auto-loading pistol in 1892, but the Hugo Borchardt pistol of 1893 was the first to have a separate magazine in the handle, a defining characteristic of such weapons. The earliest Ferdinand Mannlicher pistol was designed in 1894 to be self-loading and to use a special rimmed cartridge in 6.5 mm (.256 caliber). The weapon use an unusual blow-forward action to load an eject shells. A stripper clip (capacity five rounds) was inserted in the clip guide of the receiver and the cartridges were pressed into the magazine. The US Army tested the pistols in 1900. They did not recommend their use primarily because of the repeated failure of the ammunition.

Two of the more iconic auto-pistols of the era were the C96 "Broomhandle" Mauser (initially a bottlenecked 7.65 mm Parabellum) and the Luger (9mm Parabellum), but there were many other early designs. The "Broomhandle" Mauser, in its original 1896 configuration, had a fixed, non-removable ten-round magazine located in front of the trigger, which was loaded directly through the breech from the top of the pistol. One of the experimental formats for this pistol was the creation of a pistol-carbine with a wooden shoulder stock-holster combination for use by light cavalry. Young Lieutenant Winston Churchill was fond of the C96 Mauser and used one from horseback at the 1898 Battle of Omdurman and during the Second Boer War in Africa.

The Swiss army adopted the first Lugar pistol (developed c. 1898) in 1900, and the German Army followed in 1908. The Luger was designed to use a toggle-lock action, which uses a distinctive jointed arm to lock the chamber as opposed to the slide actions of almost every other semi-automatic pistol. The Luger pistol was manufactured to exacting standards and had a long service life. Thousands were taken home by returning Allied soldiers during both World Wars. Although outdated, the Luger is still sought after by collectors both for its sleek design and accuracy.

By the turn of the century, automatic pistols had made firm inroads into the handgun area. John Browning designed the .25 ACP (6.35 mm) cartridge in 1905 for early automatic blowback pistols that lacked a breech locking mechanism. The cartridge was designed to duplicate the performance of a .22 Long Rifle cartridge, when fired from a 2-inch barrel. The .25 caliber was the smallest diameter case Browning could use, and still utilize a center-fire primer pocket and leave sufficient rim for secure seating. It produced just the energy now cited by NATO as lethal. The .22 Long Rifle cartridges were actually more energetic (100+ ft-lbs), but their rimfire ignition was often too unreliable for defensive purposes. In the early 20th century, before firearms experts became large caliber oriented, both the .25 and the .32 calibers served well for self-defense and agency (police) ammunition especially in Europe.[45]

The Browning 1900 automatic pistol is historically noted as being among the handguns carried by Cheyenne, Wyoming, Deputy Sheriff Richard Proctor, who arrested Tom Horn for murder in 1902. New York retailer Von Lengerke & Detmold continued to import various Mauser models until around 1910, and Mauser Broomhandles were also being distributed through Browning Brothers in Ogden, Utah, Iver Johnson, and through firearms stores in many major US cities.

The Colt Model 1903 Pocket Hammerless designed by John Browning was a popular example of an early simple blowback pistol chambered in .32 ACP that had a "modern" look. The weapon was ages before its time. The resistance provided by the mass of the slide alone was enough to delay opening of the chamber until pressure in the barrel had dropped to a safe level. Approximately 570,000 Colt Pocket Hammerless pistols were produced from 1903 to 1945, in five different variants. The "hammerless" designation was merely an advertising ploy pointing out the pistol's particular suitability for concealed carry. Government General Officer models were often engraved with the officer's name.

The Winchester Model 1903 chambered in .22 long rifle was the first commercially available semi-automatic firearm made by the Winchester Repeating Arms Company. The mass of the rifle provided sufficient inertia for its reliable operation. It was produced through 1932.

A photo detail taken by Annette Ross Hume (c. 1903) clearly shows a C96 "Broomhandle" with its detachable shoulder stock among the more traditional weapons used by a posse formed by Sheriff James Thompson in Anadarko, Oklahoma Territory. A wooden shoulder stock attached via a channel in the pistol's back strap and was hollow to be used as a holster. (Photo courtesy Western History Collections, University of Oklahoma)

Actor Charles Bronson recreated a similar log cabin siege in the film *Death Hunt* (1981). The action packed thriller supposedly takes place in the Yukon Territory in 1931-1932, and was based on the attempt to arrest a real murderer Albert Johnson, known as the Mad Trapper of Rat River. No motive for his crimes has ever been established. After surrounding the cabin, a posse threw a dynamite charge into it. After the explosion collapsed the building, the men tried to rush Johnson, but he opened fire from beneath the ruins. No one was hit, but after a 15-hour standoff in −40 °F weather the posse retreated. These events and the subsequent manhunt became a media circus as Johnson eluded the Royal Canadian Mounted Police (RCMP) for 48 days in the wilderness ultimately dying of wounds received in a shoot-out. He had with him a Savage Model 99, a .30-30 caliber lever action rifle, a .22 caliber handgun, and 700 rounds of ammunition. The film reverses the facts of the case, making Johnson a sympathetic, freedom-loving character and changing RCMP hero Constable Edgar Millen from the young and popular figure, who lost his life, into a broken-down, middle-aged alcoholic played by actor Lee Marvin.

7. On Gunfighting

Gunfight Tactics

Precise shooting is difficult even when the active shooter is not also a target. Due to factors rarely encountered in the Old West such as body armor and the bolstering effect of drugs, or the more common failure to hit vital organs, the body shots may not be immediately effective, necessitating the third shot. This rapid-fire pattern of "two to the chest, one to the head" has been used in numerous TV shows and films, and in other media. However, it generally relies on the use of automatic fire rather than that of single action revolvers. The problem with shooting an adversary in the head during a gunfight is that the person is highly mobile in such a circumstance, especially after being already hit to the chest – whether or not the bullets penetrated. Another version is the body-body-hip-hip drill. With the pelvic bone shattered the victim must fall to the ground. Alternatively, one can continue shooting at the body mass until the target falls or runs away. Herein, three shots are the minimum leaving at least one round for the unexpected. This presumes that the excited shooter is keeping count! The safety-conscious shooter will leave the hammer down on an empty chamber for routine handling and carry.

It has been established, via the modern scientific investigation of life threatening situations, police combat studies, and countless videos of gunfights, that Sight Reliant Shooting (Sight Shooting), cannot be used or is not used in most real world gunfights. It should be remembered that by the middle of the 19th century most guns were capable of better accuracy than the persons shooting them. This is true today, and it can be assumed with some confidence that this circumstance was also true of encounters in the Old West. The result is the recognized and atrocious gunfight hit rate of less than 20%; which means that four out of every five bullets shot, miss the target and go somewhere else in any case. There are alternative non-sight reliant shooting methods, which are effective and could be employed to improve survivability, but the studies emphasize the observation that successful gunmen were often noted for their cold-bloodedness and outward calm demeanor during conflicts. These include Quick Kill methods and Aimed Point (Point and Shoot) methods. Both rely on the concept of *muscle memory* and require extensive practice to be effective.

In QK, the target is the focus of the shooter and is visually placed at the end of the barrel or the front site aimed only about two inches below the hit point on the target. The method has continuously repeatable results at moderate distances. Drill sergeants had an instinctive knowledge of this and constantly impressed upon their charges to aim low. In AP (P&S) close quarters situations, the chance of being shot or killed is the greatest. If that's going to happen, there is an 80% chance that it will happen at less than 21 feet. When a shooter points using the gun as an extension of the hand, he instinctively points at the feature on the object on which his eyes are focused. An impulse from the brain causes the arm and hand to stop when the finger reaches the proper position. If he changes his focus to the sights, his entire body orientation shifts also. The method can also be used without extending the arm (a.k.a. broken arm) and in situations where the sights are obscured due to bad lighting or other environmental factors. Moreover, the adrenaline dump of being in a life or death situation has been shown to adversely affect the ability of the shooter to focus on nearby objects, like gunsights. Hence, when in a gunfight the sights may be ignored. There is no need under these circumstances to go through the process of meeting those complex and must-be-met marksmanship requirements that most target shooters revere. These may be reserved for long range and sharp shooting. (US Army Field Manual 3-23.35: Combat Training With Pistols M9 and M11. June, 2003)[46]

While the velocity of a bullet affects its path and range (especially over long distances), the energy is what does the damage. In the 19th century, Colonel Townsend Whelen wrote in his very illuminating treatise, *Small Arms Design and Ballistics*, that "the thought ... was that the ideal bullet should just shoot through the animal to its opposite side, and lodge under the skin without penetrating clear through, thus expending all its energy on the beast." (p. 137) Unfortunately the conclusion reached was somewhat mistaken, or at the very least misdirected, because these views were fixated on the idea of the transfer of energy to the target, rather than on the mechanics of the work being done by the bullet in terms of wounding. The difference between efficiency and effectiveness was largely unappreciated. Naturally, at some ranges the bullet might exit with considerable residual velocity, but this wasted kinetic energy would be irrelevant if the wound was adequate. The reader should not assume from this that kinetic energy means nothing, or is somehow unrelated to wounding potential. Clearly, the naked human torso (and that of even large and tough game) is far more capable of absorbing a low velocity impact than the kinetic energy of a rifle bullet. The rate of energy transfer to the target and the location of the wound track are vastly more important than the quantity of energy transferred.

Action shooting is a set of shooting tasks where the competitors are trying to unite the three principles of precision, power, and speed, by using a period style firearm of a certain minimum power (usually measured by caliber) to score as many points as possible during the shortest amount of time. The courses are called "stages," and are shot individually by the shooters. Usually the shooter must move and shoot from several positions, fire under or over obstacles and in other unfamiliar positions. There are no standard exercises or set arrangement of the targets, and the courses are often designed so that the shooter must be inventive, and therefore the solution of exercises sometimes varies between shooters.

8. On Nuts and Bolts

Priming

The invention of the modern cartridge case rendered possible the general adoption of the breech-loading principle for all varieties of rifles, shotguns and revolvers. The development of the requisite technologies needed was hardly chronological or without drawbacks or misdirection. Most early all-metal cartridges were of the pinfire and rimfire types. Today only the small rimfires continue in use. Centerfire ammunition had been devised early in the century, but had not been perfected in terms of the reliability of ignition until about 1855. The primer was placed in the primer pocket of the cartridge. The two common centerfire primer types (Berdan and Boxer) are almost impossible to distinguish by looking at the loaded cartridge, though the two flash-holes can be seen inside a fired Berdan case and the larger single hole seen or felt inside a fired Boxer case. The Berdan primer, which uses the case as its anvil, is slightly more reliable under severe conditions but both types are more reliable than rimfire. Boxer primed cases are more easily reloaded.

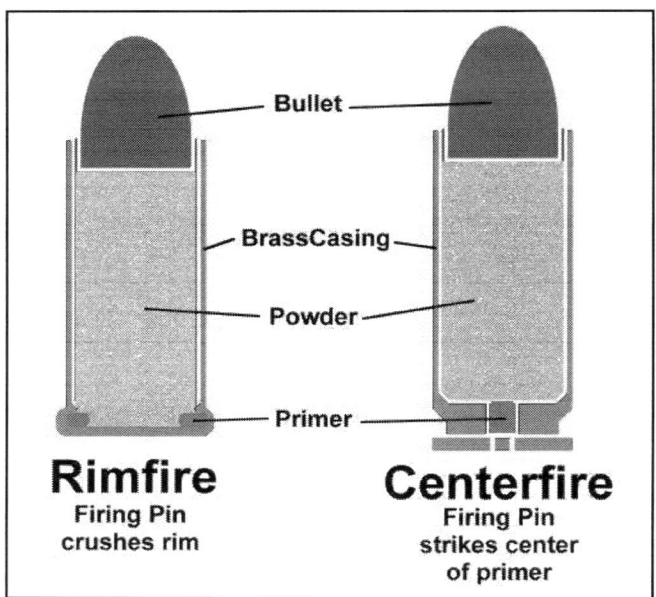

Early primers used the same mercury fulminate used in 19th century percussion caps. Black powder could be effectively ignited by hot mercury released upon decomposition. Smokeless powder, being more stable than black powder, often required more thermal energy for ignition. Incandescent particles produced by adding certain compounds of potassium to the fulminate were found most effective for igniting smokeless powder after the primary explosive gasses had heated the powder grains. The U.S. Army discontinued use of mercuric and potassium priming mixtures in 1898 mostly because they left behind a corrosive residue both in the cartridge case and in the weapon. Civilian ammunition manufacturers began offering non-corrosive primers in the 1920s.

Breechloading

By mid-nineteenth century, virtually all governments realized that they had to change from muzzle loading to breech loading firearms. The promise of government business spurred research among firearms entrepreneurs. Consumable cardboard, linen cloth, or paper cartridges with powder and ball within had been satisfactory for muzzle loading weapons, but they were fragile and subject to damage from moisture. More seriously, they were generally not adaptable to breechloaders, as they provided little or no seal for the joint between breech and barrel. Under this circumstance chamber pressures had to be carefully managed and muzzle velocity suffered. The history of breechloading is intimately connected to sealing the breech efficiently. Many cartridge designs were linked to particular weapon designs in a tail wagging the dog fashion. It is still true that a good weapon design and a good ammunition design go together.

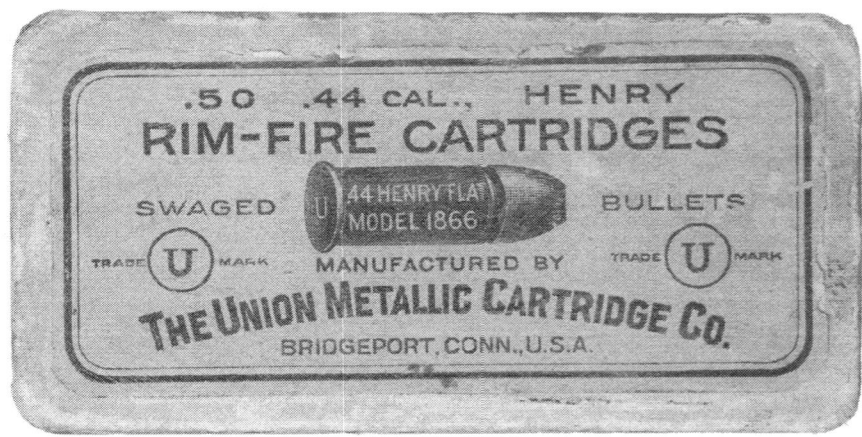

The earliest cartridge cases were of heavy brass, sealing the breech by a tapered head, like a rubber drain plug. The charge and shot were placed in a paper cylinder having a hard wad in the base. A head screw, through which the ignition passed, perforated a hole in this wad.

The efficient pinfire cartridge consisted of a thin weak shell made of brass and paper that expanded by the force of the explosion, fitting perfectly thereby into the barrel, and thus forming an efficient gas check. These cartridges were prone to damage or accidental discharge if handled improperly. So common was this circumstance that it was thought impractical to carry a pinfire weapon in a loaded condition.

Smith and Wesson came up with a practical 22 rimfire prior to 1856. A feature peculiar to this soft brass cartridge was the perforated paper base wad that restricted the priming mixture to the rim of the case, which was dented to cause ignition. The soft case also helped form a gas seal sufficient for small caliber weapons, but it was often too deformed to be reloaded.

Also in 1856, George A. Morse filed the basic U.S. patent on the features of the modern centerfire cartridge i.e., flexible metal case, crimped-in bullet, and a primer pocket in the head. His ideas, which included the rebounding firing pin, spring-loaded double-claw case extractors, and other features generally found in subsequent rifles, were far ahead of his time. Central-fire cartridges with solid-drawn metallic cases containing their own means of ignition are almost universally used in all modern varieties of military and sporting rifles and pistols.

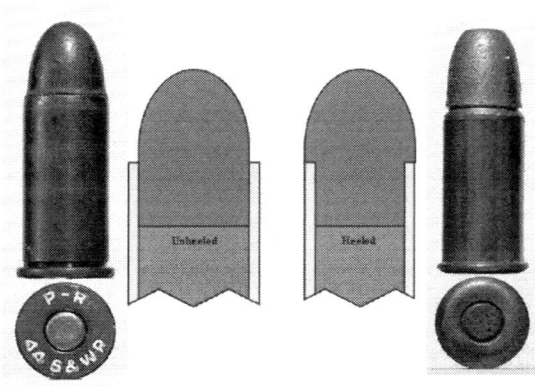

Bullets were often heeled (right) rather than crimped and some had external lubrication grooves.

Around this time, machined tolerances had improved to the point that the cartridge case was no longer necessary to seal the firing chamber of most weapons. Large rimfire cartridges were soon replaced by centerfire cartridges, which could safely handle higher pressures. This greatly streamlined the reloading procedure and paved the way for semi- and full-automatic firearms. This technological leap introduced an extra component into each round — the cartridge case — which had to be removed before the gun could be reloaded. Since the case swelled when fired, its extraction was no simple task. Nineteenth-century inventors experimented with a variety of caseless or self-consuming cartridges before finally accepting that the advantages of brass cases far outweighed any drawbacks posed by the inclusion of case extractors.

Initially, some cartridges were manufactured of rolled brass foil with an iron rim, but it was discovered that the rolled foil cartridges were prone to jamming as the barrel heated up. This was seemingly a factor in the defeat of British forces at Isandlwanda by Zulu warriors without firearms in 1879. Immediately thereafter about 4,000 Zulu warriors attacked the fortified mission station at Rorke's Drift. A mere 140 British soldiers defended the station. Fighting from prepared bulwarks made of grain sacks with virtually unlimited ammunition, they inflicted considerable casualties on the warriors and repelled the piecemeal attacks over several days. Eleven Victoria Crosses were awarded to the defenders at the station, along with a number of other decorations and honors. Nonetheless, the British Army had suffered its worst defeat against a technologically inferior indigenous foe. Previously, George Armstrong Custer (Little Big Horn 1876) had held this questionable honor. Production of cartridge cases was then switched to the drawn brass style now commonly used for the manufacture of small arms ammunition. It is safe to say that this invention completely revolutionized the art of gun making.[47]

In the Old West, the single action centerfire .45 Colt was often considered at the top of any handgun hierarchy. From a 7½-inch pistol barrel, a civilian load of black powder would easily push a 250-grain lead bullet past 900 feet per second (fps - muzzle velocity) and 460 foot-pounds of energy—a quantity derived from both mass and velocity, with the latter predominating. Yet high velocities were difficult to establish with black powder (BP) propellant. This feature of weapons design had caused firearms engineers to rely on increasing the mass of the projectile in order to increase its kinetic energy.

9. On Bullets

Bullet Types

When a bullet strikes, its high velocity and small frontal cross-section mean that it will exert large stresses in any object it hits. This usually results in it penetrating any soft object, such as flesh. The energy is then dissipated in the wound track formed by the passage of the bullet. The energy conversion efficiency of a firearm strongly depends on its construction, especially on its caliber, barrel length, and style of bullet. Nonetheless, a logical argument can be made that accuracy and penetration may outweigh bullet size and muzzle velocity in certain situations. The lethality and propriety of a round is based on many functions working together: distance, terrain, nature of the target, line of sight, objective (kill or wound), and the weight of ammunition that can be carried.[48]

Shooters today are accustomed to seeing many different bullet types and reliable load variations for any given cartridge name, but that was not the case during much of the 19th century. The Civil War saw the introduction of conical and hollow base bullets especially the style developed by Claude Minié that was used in most military muskets, but spherical lead balls were still common in revolvers. Conical bullets when loaded into cap and ball revolvers were found to be difficult to seat correctly and to have produced no notable improvement in accuracy. It should be remembered that these weapons, no matter how intimidating they appear, were designed for short range. Many cavalry exchanges in the Civil War and many gunfights in the Old West devolved into long distance exchanges of "promiscuous" and "innocent" revolver fire that were more noise than kill.

The advantage of the Minié bullet was in its ease of loading down the length of the rifled barrel of a long arm. In a revolver, the projectile needed to fit tightly in the cylinder to help prevent "chain fires" (several cylinders firing when not aligned with the barrel). Oversized lead balls were often forced into the cylinder leaving a thin ring of lead behind. The conical bullet was difficult to correctly seat in a revolver, would not have time to expand before leaving the cylinder and entering the barrel, and might take up added powder space in the cylinder, limiting velocity. Yet the conical bullet had a greater area of contact than the spherical ball with which to engage the rifling. The result was much like that of comparing a spinning football and a spinning baseball. The football and the conical bullet both have a better-defined axis of rotation with respect to the elongated shape of the projectile.

The spherical ball had a *body-centered* center of mass (COM) that minimized any tendencies toward tumbling, but any rotation not perpendicular to the path of the ball may cause unexpected discrepancies in its flight (somewhat like a screwball, curve, or sinker in a baseball pitch). These would often flatten upon impact with the target, causing a larger wound than the original diameter of the ball. The adoption of rifling allowed the use of longer, heavier bullets, but these were still typically constructed of soft lead and would often double in diameter upon impact. In these cases expansion was a side effect of materials, and there is no evidence that the bullets were designed to expand upon impact.

Conical bullets tended to suffer from tumbling in flight because their COM was asymmetrical. The placement of the COM toward the front of the hollow based Minié bullet tended to cause tumbling and key holing of wounds at longer ranges. Bullets with concentric and coincident centers of pressure and centers of mass, the use of tapered bullet heels (also known as boat-tails), and a cavity or hollow in the bullet nose (hollow point) to shift the projectile's center of mass rearwards were ultimately designed to increase precision. A bullet in which the center of pressure lies ahead of its center of mass will typically not keep its point forward orientation after impact.

Some military bullet designs have been specifically engineered to inflict more grievous wounds. The so-called Dum Dum bullets were unjacketed lead rounds produced by the Dum Dum Arsenal in India during the late 19th century. The British Army used them against native uprisings. Because the energy was roughly the same, the wounds caused by the expanding bullet of the .303 British cartridge were less severe than those caused by the larger caliber, solid lead .455 bullet used by the Martini-Henry rifle. There were several expanding bullets produced by this arsenal for the .303, including soft point and hollow point designs. These were not the first expanding bullets, however; hollow point expanding bullets were commonly used for hunting thin-skinned game in express rifles as early as the mid-1870s. Mark IV jacketed hollow point was successful enough in its first use in the battle of Omdurman (1898) that British soldiers issued with the standard bullets began to remove the top of the jacket, converting the bullets into improvised Dum Dum types.

Back in the day, some shooters notched the nose of the bullets with an incised "X" so they would flay out and cause damage similar to what hollow point rounds do today. In all likelihood this improvised notching adversely affected other factors involved in precision. Dum Dum bullets, because they were soft, expanded on impact rendering vicious wounds. They were outlawed as military rounds in 1898. Nonetheless, many law enforcement agencies around the world use hollow pointed expanding bullets on the citizens of their own country, based on the ethical fiction that there is a distinction between enemy soldiers and criminals. Nearly all rifle bullets today are pointed designs intended to deform. The typical non-deforming round nosed bullets used in the Old West generally penetrated more deeply than flat-nosed bullets, depending on the width of the flat nose and the radius of the round nose.

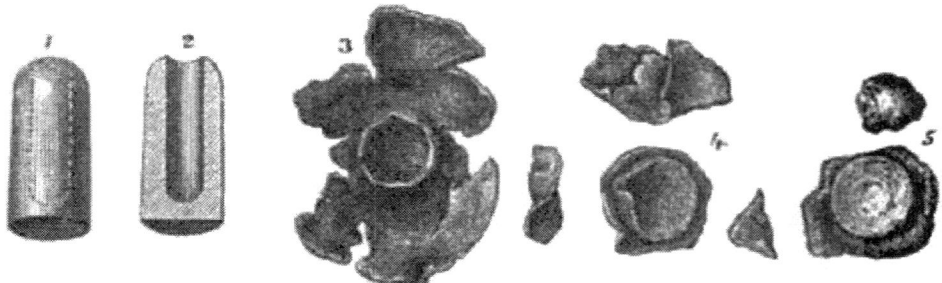

An illustration from the 1870s showing the potential fragmentation of hollow point bullets.

10. For Discreet Self Defense

The .31 caliber class of cap and ball revolvers was designed for discreet self defense. The 1849 Colt Pocket and the Remington Pocket Model were common. These small five-shot cylinders hold only about twelve grains of black powder, but they can propel a 50-grain round ball at about 700 feet per second. They were useful out to about 25 yards. The .36 caliber was developed for the U.S. Navy for shooting men without the concern of having to take down horses. It was eminently effective for the former objective, and tended to be more versatile than the .31 caliber. Service style pistols like the Remington Navy and the Colt 1851 and 1861 Navy were available to the public. Pocket varieties like the 1862 Colt Police were little more than a .31 caliber Colt blown up to take a .36 caliber round. The slightly oversized 80-grain lead balls (.375-inch diameter) for the .36 caliber could be pushed out at about 1,000 feet per second with a maximum charge of black powder. They were practical out to about 75 yards, but were capable of precise hits further out. The .44 was a popular cap and ball caliber. It started out as the huge holster pistols of the Mexican War like the big Colt Walker and Dragoon series, but evolved into more streamlined service pistols thanks to breakthroughs in metallurgy. Later service guns were like the Colt 1860 Army and the Remington New Model Army. A service gun like the 1860 Army used 30 grains of BP nominally, but the monstrous Walker was designed to hold 60 grains. The 140-grain spherical lead bullets (.451-454 caliber) could be pushed past 1,000 feet per second. The Colt Dragoon played a part in the film *True Grit* as the oversized revolver carried by little Mattie Ross with which she shoots Tom Chaney. "Everything happens to me," cries Chaney. "Now I'm shot by a child."

In 1877, Smith and Wesson introduced its black powder .38 S&W handgun cartridge with about half the energy (200-220 ft-lbs) of the common 45 Colt. The new cartridge was widely used by law enforcement for a half century in six-shot revolver duty firearms like the Colt New Police and Smith & Wesson Police. The cartridge's popularity caused manufacturers to offer smokeless powder loadings within a year of its introduction. Many inner city police chief's thought that the mild recoil of the round would increase the accuracy of law enforcement agents. [49]

The original BP .38 S&W Special was introduced in 1898 as an improvement over the BP .38 Long Colt as a military service cartridge, which was found to have inadequate stopping power against the charges of Moro warriors in the Philippines. The U.S. Army briefly reverted to using the M1873 single-action Schofield revolver in .45 Colt caliber, which had been standard during the late 19th century. The heavier bullet was found to be more effective against charging tribesmen, but the Army ultimately adopted the M1911 automatic in 45 ACP in their stead. The resulting .45 ACP lead bullet was similar in performance to the .45 Schofield revolver cartridge and only slightly less powerful (but significantly shorter) than the .45 Colt cartridge the cavalry was then using. Inventor John Browning's 1911 automatic pistol design has become one of the most successful in history. The M1911 was not replaced as the standard U.S. sidearm until 1986.

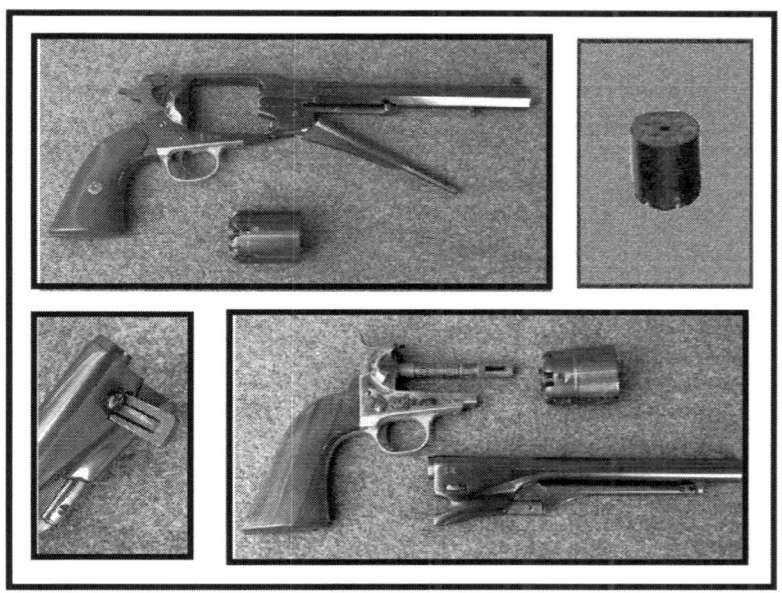

The spare cylinder (upper right) was easier to swap out in a Remington Revolver (top). There are no small or unattached parts to loose, and no tools are needed. Getting the old cylinder out and a new one in can be done more quickly than with a Colt (bottom), which demands a process of field stripping and re-assembly. The Colt wedge (lower left) is a vital component, so it was held in its slot in the barrel by a retaining screw that prevented it from falling out. A small hammer or other tool is usually needed to start and replace the wedge, and it is very easy to drop.

In 1909, a Colt-inspired revolver cartridge, then called the 38 Colt Special, introduced a flat-nosed bullet that greatly increased the stopping power of the round even at modest velocities. The 38 Smith & Wesson Special largely displaced this cartridge and was thereafter the standard service cartridge of most police departments in the United States from the 1920s to the early 1990s. Back in 1902, when the 38 S&W Special cartridge was introduced to the public, no one could have predicted what the future held for it. Almost certainly, no one would have guessed that after more than 100 years the 38 Special would be the centerfire handgun cartridge with the historically highest number of factory loadings. While it dominated until recently the double action handgun market, the 38 Special has also found a place among single action revolvers, derringers, and lever action rifles.

The velocities of bullets have generally increased with the use of a "jacket" of a metal such as copper or copper alloys that covered the massive lead core and allowed the bullet to glide down the barrel more easily than exposed lead. Jacketed bullets had been in use since at least 1882. Yet, fully jacketed bullets (FMJ) generally impart less tissue damage and more penetration than non-jacketed bullets that expand. The use of full metal jacketing in military ammunition came about because of the need for improved feeding characteristics in small arms using internal mechanical manipulation of the cartridge to chamber rounds as opposed to externally hand-reloading. In general, a bullet jacket also allows for higher muzzle velocities than bare lead without depositing significant amounts of lead metal in the bore. These bullets are designed to retain a significant portion (75%

or more) of their core to sustain penetration. This led to their adoption for military use by countries adhering to the Hague Convention in 1899.

Handgun cartridges actually made more progress than rifle ones during the years leading up to 1880. At the beginning of the previous decade ones like .44 Henry Rimfire, .44 S&W American, and .44 Colt were prevalent. With 200- to 210-grain bullets none of these would exceed about 750 fps. By 1880, these had been surpassed by .45 Colt, .44 WCF (.44-40) and .44 Russian some of which were advertised to surpass 1300 fps. Contrary to some modern anecdotes, military issue loads of BP were a bit milder under the same bullet for about 800 fps. Of course, exact powder quality and barrel fouling were confounding factors to precision.

Rifle manufacturers went all the way to .50 caliber coupled with cartridge cases in excess of 3 inches with powder capacities from 100 to 140 grains. Mostly these proved impractical for gun fighting with regard to the effects of excessive recoil. Most black powder loads seldom traveled much over 1500 feet per sec fired from a rifle. Even a fully compressed BP load had lower pressure, over a longer duration, than modern smokeless powder with its fast high pressure "spike." According to the period advertising, from the 24-inch barrel of a 1873 Winchester the company said the new .44 round would break 1,300 fps.

After the bison were exterminated the attraction of heavy-hitting calibers was greatly diminished among the gun buying public. When deer became the most common game animal nationwide, lesser caliber Winchester repeaters dominated. The Winchester rifle was also a popular weapon among gunfighters. Dubbed the "Gun that Won the West," it was widely used during the settlement of the American frontier. Shotguns were also popular weapons for "express messengers" and guards, especially those on stagecoaches and trains who were in charge of overseeing and guarding a valuable private shipment. Point and shoot, and rarely miss.

With regard to firearms, caliber (or calibre) is the approximate internal diameter of the barrel, or the diameter of the projectile it fires, in hundredths or sometimes thousandths of an inch. For example, a 45 caliber firearm has a barrel diameter of .45 of an inch. Barrel diameters can also be expressed using metric dimensions, as in a 9 mm pistol. In a rifled barrel, the distance is measured between opposing lands or grooves of the rifling. Groove-to-groove measurements are common in cartridge designations originating in the United States, while land-to-land measurements are more common elsewhere. Good performance requires a bullet to closely match the groove diameter of a barrel to ensure a good seal.

The caliber or bore diameter of smoothbore shotguns is determined by the diameter of a single ball equaling the diameter of the bore after forming a number of identically sized balls from one pound (454 grams) of lead. For a 12-gauge shotgun (0.729-inch diameter tube) the pound of lead can be formed into 12 equal sized spherical balls. For a smaller diameter tube, more balls may be cast, 20 for instance (0.615-inch diameter). Hence, the designations "12 gauge" and "20 gauge." These results can vary slightly depending on what value is used for the density of lead. The larger the gauge number the smaller the caliber of the bore.

Most 18th century firearms, including the visually intimidating pistols, fired a generally large lead ball between .63 and .75 caliber and weighing almost an ounce, but more than half a dozen different calibers were used during the Revolutionary War.

George Washington noted that most of the Patriot army's weapons were either .75 or .69 caliber (16ths and 18ths), representing common British and French military rounds, respectively. The larger British ball could be cast at a rate of 16 balls per pound of lead (1.00 ounce), while the smaller French round gave 18 balls per pound (0.92 ounce). While French ammunition could be tolerated, but lacked precision in British weapons; the reverse was not true and usually led to blocked barrels, broken ramrods, and a lot of cursing.[50]

10. On Artillery

Cannon

From about the middle of the 17th century, measurement of the bore of large gunpowder weapons (artillery) was usually expressed as the weight of its iron shot in pounds. Iron shot was used as the standard reference because iron was the most common material used for artillery ammunition during that period, and solid spherical shot the most common form encountered. Hence, the common Civil War artillery pieces termed the 20-pound smoothbore Napoleon and the 20-pound rifled Parrott Gun both fired an iron projectile having a weight of 20 pounds. Each gun had a different barrel length that affected their overall weight, designated use, and mobility. These weapons could also fire a variety of cased and exploding projectiles with different weights that fit the bore of the gun. The 20-pounder Parrott was the largest breech loading field gun used during the war, with the barrel alone weighing over 1,800 pounds. It came in two bore sizes: 2.9 inch (74 mm) and 3.0-inch (76 mm). The smaller size was much more prevalent. Confederate forces used both bore sizes during the war, which added to the complication of supplying the appropriate ammunition to its batteries. Until 1864, Union batteries used only the 2.9-inch version. The Union navy also used naval versions of the 20-, 30-, 60-, and 100-pound Parrotts. The rifled Parrott, having less windage than muzzleloaders of the same size, produced much higher internal pressures. Early models were produced with a distinctive reinforcing band at the breech. Artillery pieces often failed due to stress fatigue. In 1889, *The New York Times* called upon the Ordnance Bureau of the War Department to discontinue use of the Parrott gun altogether, following a series of mishaps and barrel failures at the West Point training grounds. Of course, most of the guns then in use for training were Civil War relics more than 25 years old.[51]

The Model 1841 Mountain Howitzer 12-pounder (sometimes termed a Prairie Howitzer) saw extended service during the Mexican–American War, the American Indian Wars, and during the American Civil War primarily in the more rugged western theaters. These small howitzers provided artillery support for forces where it would otherwise be unavailable. The original carriage design allowed the piece to be broken down into three loads for pack animal transport: the tube carried on one animal, carriage and wheels by another, and ammunition on the third. Later a Prairie Carriage was designed for traditional draft using only two horses. This versatility permitted their use with mounted forces in areas where roads were little more than paths. One of these was carried and abandoned on John C. Frémont's Second Expedition to explore and map the Oregon Trail in 1843-1844, and during the Mexican War, Lieutenant U.S. Grant placed one of these howitzers in the belfry of a church to command the nearby streets. J.E.B. Stuart, when a mere Lieutenant, had gained recognition for successfully dragging a similar piece across the West in the 1850s. Post-war, the muzzle-loading mountain howitzers defended far-flung frontier posts and supported operations against the Indians. The little howitzers soldiered on well into the 1880s. Gradually, the Army introduced the breech-loading Hotchkiss 1.65-inch Mountain Guns to replaced them. The first of 56 guns purchased by the U.S. military from the French arms firm of Hotchkiss was employed against the Nez Percé in 1877.

In some contexts, as in artillery or guns aboard a warship, "caliber" is sometimes used in combination with barrel length to describe the weapon in multiples of the bore diameter. A "5-inch 50 calibre" gun has a bore diameter of 5 inches (12.7 cm) and a barrel length of 50 times 5 inches = 250 inches (6.35 m). Complicating matters further, muzzle-loaded weapons require a significant gap between the sides of the tube bore and the surface of the shot. This was necessary so the projectile may be inserted from the mouth to the base of the tube and seated securely adjacent the propellant charge with relative ease. The gap is called windage. Early artillery barrels were short and thick, typically no longer than 26 calibers, as the gunpowder propellant they used burned very quickly and violently. Hence its acceleration time was short. Slower-burning formulations of gunpowder allowed gun barrel length to increase slightly in the 1880s, but enormous quantities of powder were required. New slower-burning "smokeless powder" propellants available from the 1880s onwards such as Poudre B, cordite and nitrocellulose allowed a more prolonged acceleration. Hence gun barrels were made progressively longer and thinner.

Horse Artillery

The Model 1841 Mountain Howitzer was one of a family of weapons designed by the US Army Ordnance Department (companion pieces were the Model 1841 12-Pdr., 24-Pdr. and 32-Pdr field Howitzers; the Model 1841 12-Pdr Gun and the 12-Pdr Mountain Howitzer). The 6-pounder Model 1841 was designed to be lightweight and highly portable. This made it possible to take cannon into mountainous or other terrain that was inaccessible for conventional artillery. Most were cast in bronze. These small Howitzers, sometimes affectionately called "bull pups," provided artillery support for forces where it would otherwise be unavailable. On roads, mountain howitzers were harnessed to a single mule. Another mule was required for its ammunition supply. When disassembled and packed on two mules, it did not require roads for transportation making it well suited to Indian fighting and mountain warfare. Mountain howitzers usually fired spherical case shot or canister ammunition. Both were shorter range, anti personnel types of ammunition than the solid 6-pound shot. Case shot was a round hollow metal shell with musket balls and a powder charge inside that had a fuse attached to detonate the powder. Canister was similar to a giant shotgun shell. Their portability made them especially suited for attachment to cavalry. Mountain howitzers set on an improved Prairie Carriage saw service during the Mexican–American War, the American Indian Wars, and during the American Civil War primarily in the more rugged western theaters.

In 1854, J.E.B. Stuart, then a newly promoted second lieutenant, arrived at Fort McIntosh in Laredo, Texas, on the Mexican border. The terrain was said to be some of the most difficult in the West. Stuart was placed in charge of the one cannon his unit possessed. During the march across the savage terrain, Stuart and his men fell behind but finally caught sight of the regiment's encampment at the bottom of a 1500-foot escarpment. To the amazement of his commanding officer comfortably ensconced below, Stuart had the cannon dismantled and lowered piece by piece by ropes down the cliff. In a letter to his brother afterward, a realization of what it means to be a soldier as well as a certain spirit shone through: "I could not and would not forsake [the artillery piece] . . . Down we went, lowering it by lariat ropes, and lifting it over rocks. We reached the bottom safely, and before night were sipping our coffee at the Major's bivouac. The Major told me that I deserved great credit for my success, and said that he never expected to see me bring the artillery down that mountain." Because of his overall performance and quite possibly in part from that spectacular feat in Texas, Stuart was selected for the new 1st Cavalry forming at Fort Leavenworth, Kansas. [52]

The 1841 Model 6-pounder Howitzer proved the equivalent of parallel European designs for infantry and cavalry support but was all but useless against fortifications. Yet these cannon were greatly feared by Native Americans who had no parallel device to make an answer to them. The cannon could fire with remarkable lethality from more than 1000 yards, well outside the effective range of most rifles, and spread lethal fragments over a 100-yard radius. The Model 1841 was slowly phased out in the 1870s and replaced by the breech loading Hotchkiss Model 1875. Its ammunition was self contained and available as canister and High Explosive (HE) nose fused shells. The army purchased 56 of these by 1898 when it was declared obsolete and relegated to militia units. The latter weapon served with cavalry units during the late American Indian Wars, including against the Nez Perce in 1877 and at Wounded Knee in 1890, and was used during the Spanish–American War and Philippine–American War. The Model 1875 broke down into two loads for mule transport. Another mule was required for its ammunition (72 rounds).

11. Military Weapons

The US Army at mid-century was essentially a frontier Army. To the defense of the frontier were added the policing of the slavery dispute in the Kansas-Missouri region, military occupation of the unreconstructed southern states, neutralization of the French in Mexico under Maximilian and of the Fenians (Irish Brotherhood) in Canada in the Northeast, and dispersion of white marauders in the Border States. But the conflict with the Native American was the overriding consideration. Many of these conflicts occurred during and after the Civil War through 1890. However regions of the West such as Texas, New Mexico, Utah, Oregon, California, and Washington, saw significant conflicts prior to 1860. When regular Army units were withdrawn to fight the Civil War in the East, the state and territorial governments raised volunteer infantry and cavalry to replace them in the West.

In terms of firearms and other weapons, the Civil War wrought a great technical change from the single shot cap and ball pistol and muzzle loading long rifle to the revolver and the repeating rifle. Swords and lances devolved from utilitarian to largely ceremonial. The officials charged with ammunition supply steadfastly spoke out against rapid-fire weapons for the military, however, because they feared that troops would run out of rounds at a rate greater than they could be supplied. The Mexican War vindicated many of the institutional forms, organizational structures, and military doctrines taught at West Point and other military academies, and their apparent success against a second-class army ensured that both sides in the Civil War would follow them dutifully.

In fact, the expansion of the United States and the military occupation of the American West during the late 1840s had increased transportation costs of the army more than fifteen times and threaten budgetary shortages elsewhere. Because of a shortage of gunpowder in 1856, the chief of ordnance ordered the powder to be removed from the large supply of paper pistol cartridges and remade to load rifle cartridges. Also, to save powder, the paper rifle cartridges were to be filled with only 50 grains of powder instead of the usual 60 leaving some firearms underpowered and forcing marksmen to adjust their point of aim. A slow moving bullet has not only a more limited lethal range, but also a much steeper trajectory. It makes a huge arc through the air. The relatively slow moving bullets (up to 40 percent slower than modern ones) produced for the attackers standing 600 yards away a safe-zone under the apex of the arc of between 200 and 300 yards in depth, or half the theoretical field of fire as measured from the shooter, where the bullets passed harmlessly high over the heads of the attackers.

Studies suggest that the so-called primary killing zone was about 100 yards deep immediately in front of the defensive position with a secondary killing zone beginning about 300 yards further out and shrinking in lethality until it reached the practical limit of the range of the weapon. At the extreme lethal range of the rifled musket (900 yards), the theoretical deadly space was only 12 yards deep with the slow moving bullets falling almost vertically, and the likelihood of hitting a human target even if the shooter knew how to correct his aim became extremely small. It was the lethal efficiency of the rifled artillery and the highly efficient versions of the exploding shells designed by a British officer, Henry Shrapnel, in the previous century, however, that were responsible for 40 percent of all Civil War battlefield casualties. Filled with small iron or lead balls and fitted with a time fuse, the Shrapnel container burst open during its passage over the enemy position giving the effect of an oversized shotgun fired from overhead. [53]

With the exception of the cavalry, who were provided with a wide assortment of innovative firearms including revolving pistols and rapid-fire repeaters, both Federal and Confederate armies issued a muzzle-loading rifled musket with percussion cap ignition that was common to period infantry through much of Europe. The percussion cap system had been adopted in the US in 1842 to replace the standard flintlock. These rifles were considerably more accurate than the previously issued muskets but were not as accurate as the American long rifle. A large number of conversions were available during the Mexican War. Most commonly they were American made .58 caliber Springfields or British .577 caliber Enfields. Both weapons could be fitted with a socket bayonet. The Federal soldiers found the Enfield more accurate and reliable than the Springfield.

The introduction of these long-range rifled muskets – considered an improvement in infantry weapons over the old smoothbores – has been identified as the cause of the mass casualties characteristic of Civil War battles where linear tactics were used. Military theorists nonetheless recognized that modern rifled weapons in the hands of the infantry made the cavalry charge and the frontal infantry assault impractical. The old shock tactics, highly successful against infantry armed with smoothbore muskets effective at only 100 yards, would be suicidal against entrenched troops whose firearms were deadly at 800. See Rifling below.

Antebellum development

The arms and weapons of the Alamo defenders of 1836 were widely varied. Hollywood films portray all the men as buckskin-clad frontiersmen armed with their Kentucky or Pennsylvania long rifles. The truth is most of the men used what they had. Some were issued Mexican arms from the stores of guns captured after General Cos surrendered at the Battle of Bexar in December 1835. The arms and equipment that had been captured by the Texans included: 816 muskets, rifles, and pistols, 200 bayonets, 21 cannon, 14,600 cartridges and large numbers of solid shot and canister. Texans found the Mexican powder to be of such low quality that many considered it useless. The poor quality powder created a large amount of fouling in the barrel that impeded the loading of subsequent shots. To compensate for this, soldiers were issued undersized soft lead balls.

The Mexican Escopeta was a short smoothbore musket or carbine that was a popular weapon of the 18th century using the Spanish Miguelet lock, a very durable system that was still being used in the southwest many decades later. In the mid 1820s, Mexico bought a large number of British arms and issued these to its regulars and active militia battalions. Some of the muskets bought by the Mexicans came with a socket bayonet, others with a sword bayonet or a plug bayonet. The last was similar to a long handled knife shoved into the barrel to create a spear but effectively making the weapon useless as a firearm. There is evidence that suggests that Mexico armed its infantry with the British East India Pattern musket, a 39-inch barrel of .75 caliber, a cheaply made version of the famous "Brown Bess." Both Fusileros (fusiliers used as line infantry) and Granaderos (grenadiers used as picked troops and reserves) were similarly armed. Besides being Britain's main infantry weapon in the Napoleonic Wars and the expansion of its Indian empire, this musket saw use on every continent. Mexico did not arm its

Cazadores (light infantry used as the battalion skirmishers or flankers) with the standard infantry musket. Like many light infantries of the day, the Cazadores used light infantry muskets that fired a .63 caliber ball. A few carried the British Baker rifle, also .63 caliber and probably the best-made arm carried by the Mexican forces.

Some among the Alamo defenders may have used imported sporting weapons. The hunter carried his long rifle while farmers and tradesmen probably used shotguns and fowlers. Most shotguns can fire undersized musketballs (10 gauge .77 caliber, 12 gauge .73, 20 gauge .63). The US Musket Model 1816 had enjoyed the highest production run of any military flintlock produced by the United States, and the flintlock US Common Rifle of 1817 was widely in use by 1836. The flintlock was the more established ignition system, yet there were probably more cap locks involved in the siege than is currently acknowledged.

The defenses at the Alamo had been designed to withstand an attack by infantry, not an artillery-equipped army. The Mexican artillery included several 8-lb, 6-lb, and 4-lb cannon, mortars, and 7-inch howitzers stationed in batteries on three sides of the Alamo. Muddy roads delayed two 12-pound guns that would have demolished the defending walls. During the first week of the siege over 200 Mexican cannon shots landed in the Alamo plaza. The Texians often picked up the cannonballs and reused them in the 21 guns belonging to the defenders including a massive 18-pounder. The reluctance to abandon such a precious store of artillery may have played an important role in the decision to remain at the Alamo. Based on recent research, 18 cannon of various sizes have been identified: the famous 18-pounder, one iron 16-pounder, one iron 12-pound gunnade, one 9 inch pedrero that fired stone balls, two iron 8-pounders, six 6-pounders, three iron 4-pounders, another 4-pounder of either brass or bronze and two 3-pounders. If strict military doctrine had been followed nearly half the garrison would have been assigned to the artillery. A lack of powder and the need to man the walls prevented this.

After the siege had ended, at least 13 cannon were spiked and had their cascabals and trunions broken off before being dumped in the ditches around the compound. An unknown number of bronze and brass cannon were melted down or taken back to Mexico successfully putting an end to the Alamo Artillery. At San Jacinto some months later, two cannon, a gift from some citizens of Cincinnati known as the "Twin Sisters," played a significant role in the Mexican defeat. They must have been mobile artillery, but no one seems to know definitively what the Twin Sisters looked like. The Cincinnati foundry that manufactured the guns had no record detailing their specifications, and several pairs of iron and brass 6-pounders seemed to have been identified as being honored in cities in Texas.

A decade later, in the effort to join the Texas Republic to the United States, the Mormon Battalion (about 550 men officially called the 1st Iowa Volunteers) was mustered into service (July 1846) as part of the Army of the West under US General Stephen Watts Kearny. Its service during the Mexican War supported the eventual cession of much of the American Southwest from Mexico to the United States. Besides Kearny's own 300 troopers of the 1st Dragoons, the Army of the West consisted of 1600 men in the volunteer First and Second Infantry Regiments of Fort Leavenworth; the Missouri Mounted Cavalry regiment under Alexander Doniphan; an artillery battalion; and the Mormon volunteers. Eventually the Army of the West would have some 4,000 soldiers operating in California, New Mexico, and Mexico. Kearny was one of the foremost officers of the United States Army on the antebellum frontier. Commander of the Army's Third Military Department, which was charged with protecting the frontier and preserving peace among the tribes of Native Americans on the Great Plains, he is considered the father of the US Cavalry.

During its service, the Mormon Battalion made a grueling march of nearly 2,000 miles from Council Bluffs, Iowa, to San Diego emphasizing the sometimes-overlooked role of infantry on the frontier. For the most part the Mormon soldiers went to war in civilian clothing. They were issued knapsacks, haversacks, and canteens. Tents, cooking gear and supplies were hauled in wagons. There is documented evidence that Ordnance Department personnel at Fort Leavenworth issued the Mormon Battalion with three different types of infantry weapons, a flintlock smoothbore musket - Model 1816, a flintlock rifle - Model 1803, and a percussion cap rifle, possibly a .69 conversion or alternatively the .54 caliber Model 1841. These fired a round ball that was essentially the same as that used in the Revolution. Mormon volunteers were promised that they could keep their arms and equipage once their twelve-month term of service had been completed. These weapons may have formed the core of those used by the later Nauvoo Legion to police the Mormon settlements in the West. All these are represented today in the LDS Museum of Church History and Art in Salt Lake.

The Model 1841, called the "Mississippi Rifle," owes its nickname to the successful use of this weapon by a Mississippi regiment under the command of Jefferson Davis in the Mexican War. Many older Mississippi rifles of .54 caliber were later re-bored to .58 caliber so that they could use the .58 caliber Minié Ball that had become the government standard. Purchased as surplus, it became a great favorite among frontier emigrants. Thousands of surplus or condemned military arms were sold at auction, usually to large wholesalers. Some of these guns were original flintlocks from the early days of the nation, some were flintlocks converted to the percussion system, and some were outdated original percussion arms. Whatever their ages, they were inexpensive and at least marginally reliable. A listing of arms in one government sale at Fort Leavenworth reportedly appeared in the *Daily Times* (31 May 1860).

In 1855, the government had issued a US Model 1855 musket, which was the first to fire the .58 conical Minié Ball. The hollow base of the conical projectile improved both loading time and accuracy. When the rifle was fired, the expanding gas pushed forcibly on the base of the bullet, deforming it to engage the rifling. This provided spin for accuracy, a better seal for consistent velocity and longer range, and some cleaning of barrel fouling. The Minié ball tended to cut a straight path and usually went all the way through the injured part; the ball seldom remained lodged in the body. If a Minié ball struck a bone, it usually caused the bone to shatter. The Model 1855 also came with a Maynard tape primer (somewhat like a child's roll of caps for a toy). This system was designed by Edward Maynard to allow for more rapid reloading. Maynard also developed an automatic feeding system that would advance the tape when the musket's hammer was cocked. The tape worked well under controlled conditions, but proved to be unreliable in the field. Fortunately, the standard copper caps could also be used. The weapon is best remembered for its service with the 7th New York Volunteers in the eastern theater. In 1862, the California militia (as part of the Department of the Pacific: 1st – 8th plus the 1st Nevada Infantry regiments) were armed with these weapons. The department had been issued 85,000 rounds of Minie ball and 40,000 additional rounds were packed on the ordinance train. At Apache Pass, the 1st and 5th regiments had several severe skirmishes, not with Confederates, but with the Apache. At least two of the militiamen were killed.

In 1846, Kearny with 300 men of the 1st Dragoons mounted mostly on durable mules led his command into the desert toward California intent on winning the territory for the United States. With his men mounted on weary untrained animals, he executed an uncoordinated attack on a force of Mexican lancers who were mounted on well-trained horses. The lancer had become a common sight in almost every European army. Kearny's column, along with the small force of Marines and volunteer militia, suffered a defeat. Nonetheless, the remaining Mexican military forces retreated without further fighting, and Kearny's forces easily took control of New Mexico. He left three companies of Dragoons to form, with volunteer troops, a strong garrison in New Mexico under Sterling Price. In the Siege of Los Angeles, a company of lancers temporarily recaptured the town, expelling a company of US Marines. It is conjectured that a band of Mexican cavalry killed a volunteer American chaplain, Father Anthony Rey, as his body was discovered, pierced by lances. Father Rey, formerly a pastor in Georgetown, Maryland, had gone forward alone from Matamoras in order to minister to some wounded among the Mexicans at Ceralvo. [54]

As the ranking Army officer in the Southwest, Kearny had claimed command of California at the end of hostilities despite the fact that California was brought under US control by Commodore Robert F. Stockton's (USN) Pacific Squadron and John C. Fremont's volunteer California Battalion composed of hunters, scouts, mission Indians, and armed citizens including Kit Carson (enrolled as a Lieutenant). The latter generally furnished their own ammunition and other equipment for the expedition. Most of these were practiced riflemen. Attached to the battalion were two pieces of artillery, under the command of Lieutenant McLane, of the navy. A Kentucky newspaper editor who was present noted: "In the appearance of our small army there is presented but little of the pomp and circumstance of glorious war ... A leathern girdle surrounds the waist, from which are suspended a Bowie and a hunter's knife, and sometimes a brace of pistols. These, with the rifle and holster-pistols, are the arms carried by officers and privates." [55]

A second Federal unit called the Regiment of Mounted Riflemen (1st Mounted Rifles) was authorized by an act of Congress in May 1846 to protect emigrants on the Oregon Trail, but it was deployed instead to Mexico where it served with distinction especially in the attack on Chapultepec. After the Mexican War, the unit was stationed at Jefferson Barracks, Missouri and Fort Merill, Texas. Unfortunately, the companies of the 1st Mounted Rifles were widely scattered and the number of troops available was wholly inadequate for the task of patrolling an area that extended from Colorado to the Mexican border, and from Kansas to Utah. In 1855, Secretary of War Jefferson Davis organized two new cavalry regiments (not Dragoons or Mounted Rifles). They were to be elite, with handpicked officers. In the first military bill passed by Congress after the start of the Civil War, only one regiment was added to the regular Federal cavalry.

The few regiments of cavalry that existed in the regular army were initially broken up into small detachments for the purpose of ranging the Western frontiers, with a few squadrons patrolling between the outposts carrying messages from camp to camp or pompously escorting the commanding generals in their grand reviews and parades. The Federal hierarchy did not add substantially to the mounted arm until embarrassed by Southern cavaliers at First Bull Run in 1861. Among these additional mounted units were the 9th and 10th Cavalry composed of black troopers (Buffalo Soldiers) sent west specifically to fight Indians. The Federal cavalryman was usually armed with a sword, a single-shot carbine, and one revolver, giving him a total of seven shots without reloading.

Military Long arms

The emergence of new, innovative firearms notwithstanding, conservative US Ordnance officials initially decided against the cavalry breechloader and chose to equip mounted troops with an old-fashioned smoothbore muzzleloader. Adopted in 1847, the .69 caliber percussion Cavalry Musketoon was actually a shortened version of the excellent Model 1842 Infantry Musket. The 1847 Cavalry Musketoons came in for a fair share of criticism, however. The ramrod proved a particular disadvantage on horseback. It needed (but did not receive) a retaining spring on the underside of the barrel or a British-style articulated swivel "to keep the ramrod from falling out." Moreover, troopers found that the bullets (undersized to insure easy loading on horseback) had a tendency to move dangerously forward in the barrel during field service. The guns were loaded with a round ball contained within a paper cartridge, and the jouncing of a cavalry mount caused the load to unseat, particularly when the carbines were carried on the saddle muzzle-down. Troopers often carried this weapon across the pommel of their saddles or muzzle up with the buttstock on their thigh. Some 1847 Musketoons were later rifled and fitted with adjustable rear sights. More than 6,000 Cavalry Musketoons were made between 1847 and 1859, and many served in the first years of the Civil War at which time the military embraced the breechloader, primarily in the guise of the superb Sharps system. The often-repeated story of boxes of rifles being marked "bibles" by Rev. Henry Ward Beecher to prevent their detection by proslavery forces in Kansas has imparted the name "Beecher's Bibles" to Sharps rifles.

The "falling block" on this early Sharps Carbine is open. Later models were more vertically oriented. Some models came with an automatic capping mechanism, the caps in rolls of thin copper (bottom right) similar to paper caps used in 1950s toy guns. The paper wrapped conical round is at the top.

Occasionally, the Federal ordnance department tested new weapons. In 1856, the ordnance department sent sixty-four Sharps Carbines to New Mexico to be tested by troops in the field. The Sharps was being considered as a possible replacement for the Musketoon. The weapons were distributed among the mounted riflemen who were charged with gathering reports on its performance. The troops involved in testing the Sharps found the carbines to be "greatly preferred as an arm for the Dragoon service." The weapon was adopted and was popular among mounted troops before and during the Civil War. An experimental "double breached Pistol" was tested at about the same time in New Mexico and found to be "of no account." The most widely produced revolving rifle was the Model 1855 based on the .44 caliber Army revolving pistol. An estimated total of only 4,435 were manufactured in the Hartford factory (c. 1856–1864). A few Colt revolving rifles were issued to some of the mounted riflemen in New Mexico in 1859. It was not recorded what the troops or their officers thought of the Colt weapons, but the Department Commander ordered them turned in to the ordnance depot. A supply of 20 Wesson (of Smith and Wesson) rim fire rifles was also tested "for some special purpose," but the department stated that the weapons then in the hands of the mounted riflemen would not be changed. The army was slow to change because of the inertia built into the highly bureaucratic system and, perhaps more importantly, because it cost money to switch, money that Congress was disinclined to spend during peacetime. [56]

The evolution of the cavalry carbine as a service weapon was rapid during the war, and many different makes were available. The Massachusetts Arms Company was formed in 1857 for the purpose of producing Dr. Maynard's breech loading long arms. The guns were produced in both carbine and rifle lengths, with 20 and 26 inch barrels respectively, and were offered in .35 and .50 caliber as well as a 20 gauge shotgun. The Maynard's ease of operation and ability to function quickly and reliably helped to win the Massachusetts Arms Company a contract for 400 of their .50 military pattern carbines.

Also in 1857, the Burnside carbine, designed and patented by (General) Ambrose Burnside in 1853, won a competition at West Point against 17 other carbine designs. The unique, cone-shaped and reloadable Burnside cartridge sealed the joint between the barrel and the breech that tended to leak hot gases when fired in other breechloaders. Burnside's design generally eliminated this problem. The trigger guard doubled as a lever that dropped the breechblock swinging up the cartridge chamber for easy drop in loading.

The acceptance of the carbine induced Burnside to briefly leave the army (although he remained in the state militia) and to establish extensive factories for its manufacture in Bristol, RI. With the outbreak of the Civil War, the federal government ordered over 55,000 of these weapons making it the third most popular carbine of the war. Only the Sharps carbine and the Spencer carbine were more widely used. It has been estimated that more than forty Federal cavalry regiments were using the Burnside carbine during the 1863-1864 period. Additionally, seven Confederate cavalry units were at least partially armed with the weapon during this same period.

The development of the breech-loading rifled carbine was a significant advance in cavalry arms—the best known probably being the Sharps Carbine of which 150,000 were made. Sharps rifles have been historically renowned for long range and high accuracy (effective range about 500 yards under perfect conditions). The carbine was chambered for a .52 caliber lead projectile. This slightly smaller bullet imparted less recoil to the less massive carbine than the .58 caliber ammunition used in heavier infantry arms. The Confederates produced a clone of this "falling block" weapon called the Richmond Carbine (5,400 weapons) for their own forces because it used a simple paper cartridge and percussion cap.

The Sharp's Rifle (a longer version of the carbine) had been developed during the war as a possible infantry weapon, but it was never adopted as anything other than a weapon for sharpshooters. These rifles were renowned for long-range accuracy. The government ordnance department made many tests including variations in muzzle velocity and penetration of lead bullets through one-inch target boards and into sand. The falling block action invented by Christian Sharps lent itself to conversion to the new metallic cartridges developed in the late 1860s, and many of these converted carbines were used during the Indian Wars. This rifle was one of the few successful designs to transition to metallic cartridge use. By 1874 the rifle was available in a variety of calibers and had been adopted by the armies of a number of nations.

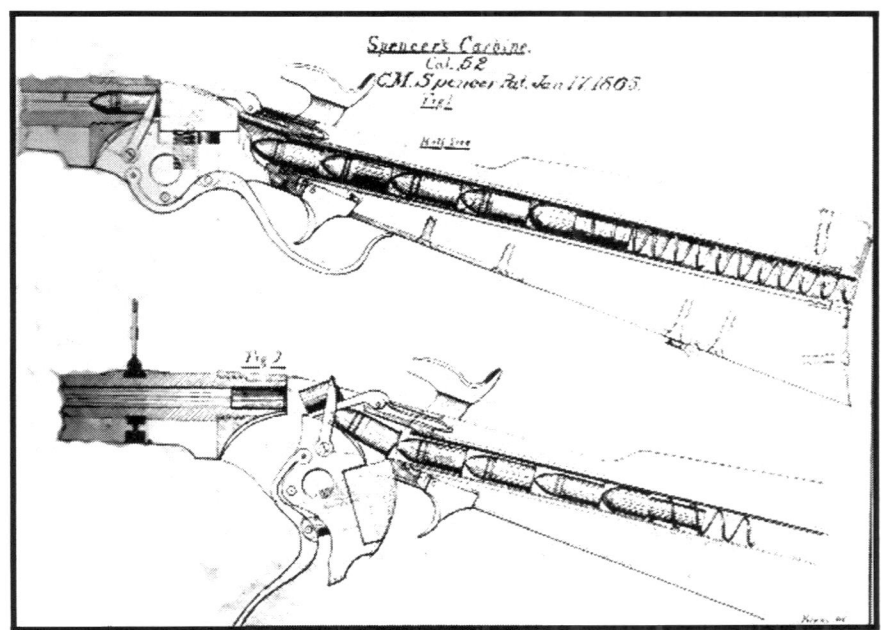

The operation of the Spencer magazine can be seen in its Patent application. Often, Federals with Spencer's fired only one shot together to simulate a volley of musketry and waited for the Confederates to advance. When they did, the Unionists unleashed the other six shots in a rapid fusillade of fire that devastated the Southern lines.

Rifling

While a smoothbore musket could be made to expel a solid ball with a greater muzzle velocity than a rifle musket, it was the projectile that the latter weapon fired – the slightly smaller Minié ball – that made all the difference. Minié balls were made smaller in diameter than the inside of the barrel, so they could be inserted more easily. When fired, the base of the bullet expanded and gripped the rifle grooves, which imparted a spiral on the projectile and thereby gave it its greater range and accuracy. British soldiers engaging Bantu tribesmen in Africa in 1852 had noted the improved accuracy of their weapons and "were amazed to discover that Bantu could be picked off at up to thirteen hundred yards, or at least four times the extreme range of smoothbore muskets." [57]

Popularized during the Crimean War, it was perfected in early 1850s America. A gunsmith at the arsenal in Harpers Ferry named James Burton had simplified the design that had made the Minié famous and developed a hollow-based, .58-caliber lead projectile that could be cheaply mass produced. Unlike a spherical ball, which could pass through the human body nearly intact, leaving an exit wound not much larger than the entrance wound, the soft, hollow-based Minié ball flattened and deformed upon impact, creating a shock wave that emanated outward. If the ragged, tumbling bullet had enough force to cleave completely through the body, which it often did, it tore out an exit wound several times the size of the entrance wound. As the *Cincinnati Lancet and Observer* noted following the Union victory at Gettysburg: "Our readers will not fail to have noticed that everybody connected to the army has been thanked, excepting the surgeons."[58]

Due to the high cost of precision manufacturing especially on the inside of the barrel, and the need to load quickly from the muzzle, the spherical musket ball was a loose fit in the barrel. Consequently, on firing, the ball bounced off the sides of the barrel when fired and the final direction on leaving the muzzle was unpredictable. At the battle of Batoche in 1885, the Metis in Canada held off government forces until the rebels ran out of lead balls. Those that still held their positions resorted to hunting in the underbrush for bullets fired by government troops and firing them back, and some fired nails and round pebbles from a nearby streambed instead of bullets from their rifles. The stones were seen to curve in their flight rising or falling, turning right or left randomly, and sometimes hitting targets taking cover behind trees and fortifications. This story emphasizes the need for precision when utilizing a firearm.

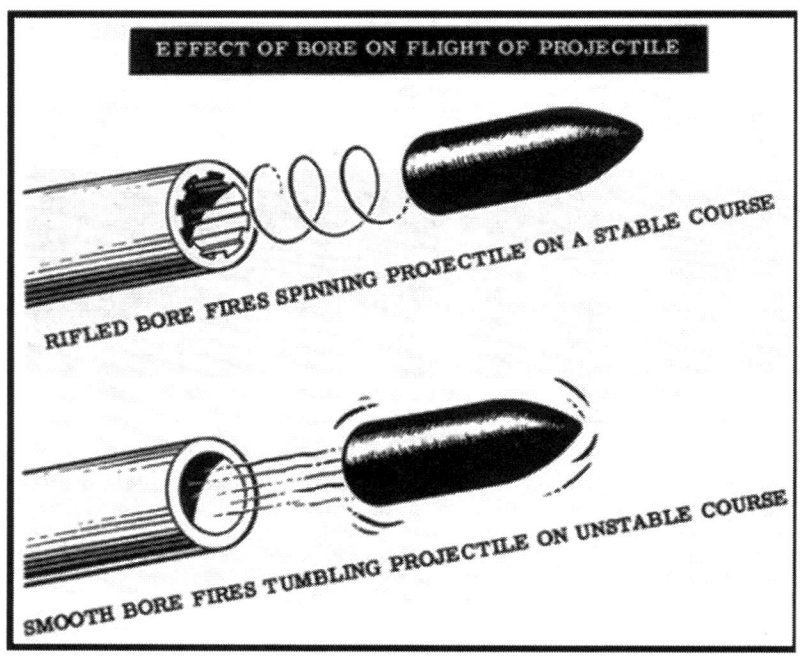

The concept of stabilizing the flight of a projectile by spinning it was known in the days of bows and arrows when the feathers were offset to produce rotation, but early firearms using black powder had difficulty with rifling because of the fouling left behind between the lands and grooves by the combustion of the powder. The expanding base of the Minié ball allowed for a more precise fit. This spin serves to gyroscopically stabilize the projectile, improving its stability and accuracy.

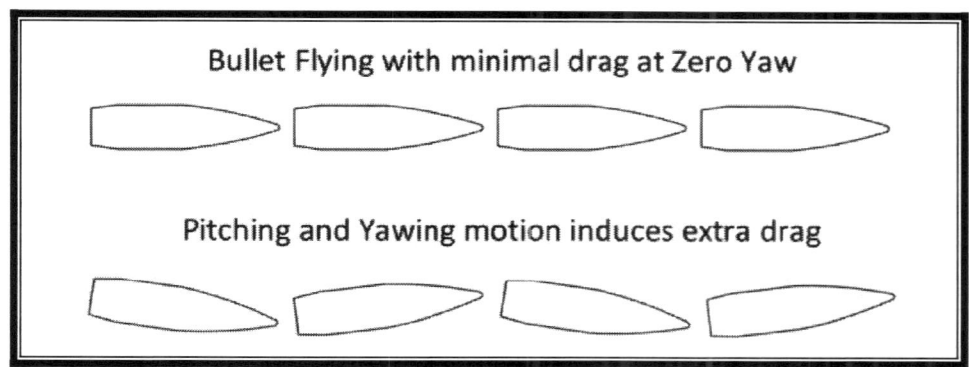

Many modern manufacturers use a 1:20 twist to travel ratio in the rifling, but there is a report from 1879 saying better results were achieved with a tighter 1:18. For example, 1:10 twist is, 1 complete bullet revolution every 10 inches of barrel length traveled. A shorter travel distance indicates a "faster" twist, meaning that for a given velocity the projectile will be rotating at a higher spin rate. If an insufficient twist rate is used, the bullet will begin to yaw and then tumble, hitting the target at an angle.

Of course, for a spherical ball, this makes little difference, but the proper spin helps stabilize its flight. It is only necessary that the poles of the rotating sphere remain pointed along the trajectory of the projectile. For elongated bullets, bullet yaw is significant. Once the bullet starts to yaw, any hope of accuracy is lost, as the bullet will begin to veer off in random directions like a poorly struck golf ball or a properly thrown "curve ball" pitch in baseball. The combination of length, weight and shape of a projectile determines the twist rate needed to stabilize it – barrels intended for short, large-diameter projectiles like spherical lead balls require a very low twist rate, such as 1:48; for barrels intended for long, small-diameter bullets, as tight as 1:8. The so-called centrifugal force of a spinning bullet helps to expand it when the bullet impacts a solid object.

The optimal twist in the rifling seems also to be link to the aspect ratio (length/diameter) of the bullet as well as its mass. Consequently, a light weight bullet spinning with excessive speed will lose more energy to the environment in flight due largely to friction with the air. Air resistance increases with the square of speed, hence a bullet moving or spinning twice as fast experiences four times the friction, three times as fast - nine times the friction, and so on. A good rule of thumb is that the heavier and longer a bullet is, the faster the rifling twist rate needs to be to stabilize it in flight. A too-high rate of twist can also cause problems like accelerated barrel wear. Common twist ratios for the popular 30-30 Winchester (150 grains round nose lead) are approximately 1:12. The tighter twist also seemed to impart a long range advantage for shooting heavier bullets (500 grains). In some cases, rifling will have twist rates that increase down the length of the barrel, called a *gain twist* (*progressive twist*). Gain twist rifling was used as early as the Civil War (1861–65). Colt Army and Navy revolvers both employed gain twist rifling. Gain twist rifling, however, is more difficult to produce than uniform rifling, and the weapons are, therefore, more expensive to manufacture.[59]

The Spencer Rifled Carbine was the most "modern" military weapon to see widespread use in the Civil War. Of the 145,000 Spencer's made, the Federal Government acquired 110,000 during the war. It became the most popular of the rifled carbines for cavalry use by the Union Army, and was widely used in the West after the Civil War. The design was for a tube style magazine-fed, lever-operated rifle chambered for a rimfire cartridge. Operation of the lever also ejected the spent cartridge case. The actual bullet diameter was also .52 inches. The rim fire design (like a modern .22 caliber) was a great advantage when mounted. The rim fire cartridge removed one step (that of placing a percussion cap in place) from the readying sequence. When empty, the tube magazine could be rapidly reloaded either by dropping in fresh cartridges one by one or from a device called the Blakeslee Cartridge Box, which contained up to thirteen reloading tubes with seven cartridges in each, which could be emptied into the magazine tube through the buttstock. With a supply of 98 cartridges (7 in the gun and 91 in the box), the common joke was "Load it on Sunday and shoot all week." However, the rim fire cartridge could not be reloaded, leading to the development of center fire ammunition.

At Gettysburg, 3 million rounds of small arms ammunition was expended by all forces over three days producing fewer than 60,000 casualties, requiring 50 musket shots to produce one hit on the enemy (a 2 per cent efficiency of fire) even if all those wounded or killed by artillery, bayonets, and edged weapons during the battle are totally ignored. A number of period studies regarding the Crimean War of the previous decade had shown that 60 rounds was the average used by a soldier shooting a rifle all day at appropriate targets. A properly trained soldier, therefore, managed in theory only to take out his opposite number in a full day's fighting—a grinding mutual attrition also characteristic of the American Civil War that may have added to the overall indecisiveness of its combat.[60]

Nearly all Civil War and prewar ammunition was issued as paper cartridges. Neither loose ammunition components nor metal cartridges were common. The paper was impregnated with nitrate salts to make it combustible. The first successful metallic copper cartridge was invented just before the American Civil War and saw limited use, but it was too soft to be repeatedly reused and required a supply chain too open to disruption for its widespread use during the Civil War. Carrying enough ammunition by horse and wagon to keep a line of troops armed with Spencer carbines firing merrily away may well have been beyond the available capability of the time. In the Civil War, the goal was for muzzle loading infantry to go into battle with about 40 paper wrapped rounds apiece in their cartridge boxes and 20 rounds in reserve in their kit (at 11 to 12 shots per pound for 4 to 6 pounds). Details of men were often obliged to go to the ammunition wagons, break open the boxes, and carry the cartridges in blankets to supply the men along the line. No battle of the Civil War has been found to have been lost due to a lack of ammunition.

Tactical strength under most battlefield conditions proved to be, not in the effective range of the cavalry weapon (for pistols about 30 yards) or the number of men firing them, but in the number of shots that could be delivered without time consuming reloading. Troopers became less aggressive once they went into reloading mode.

In December 1866, for example, Captain William J. Fetterman went out with 80 men to relieve a party of woodcutters ostensibly under attack by a small party of Sioux. The soldiers at Fort Phil Kearny had been tasked with protecting immigrants traveling to the gold fields of Montana Territory along the Bozeman Trail. Fetterman decided to carry the fight to the Indians and rode out of sight of the fort in pursuit. The small party proved to be a decoy, and Fetterman and all his men were killed in an ambush. The Indians wiped out the entire force, including two civilians who had gone along to try out their new Henry repeating rifles, weapons far superior to the Springfield muzzle-loaders carried by the infantrymen and the few Spencer carbines and revolvers carried by the cavalrymen in the detail.

In the Hayfield Fight in August 1867, a detachment of 19 soldiers and 6 civilians, making hay for the fort under Lt. Sigismund Sternberg, equipped with converted breech-loading Springfields and several repeating rifles, held off vastly superior odds with a loss of only 3 killed and 3 wounded. Again in August, Red Cloud attacked a party of 14 woodcutters' wagons under the command of Capt. James W. Powell. Once alerted, Powell formed an enclosure of wagon boxes and prepared to repulse the attack of more than 100 mounted warriors. The Indians had learned to attack whites in successive waves, the first to draw their fire and the second to close before the standard muzzleloader could be reloaded, yet on this day the Indians attacked again and again, each time receiving undiminished fire from the wagon-box enclosure. The Indians were repulsed with great loss of life. It seems that Powell's men were armed with breech-loading Springfield rifles, which had been developed at the end of the Civil War. These could be loaded almost as quickly as they were fired, using a new .50 caliber self-contained cartridge. There is no doubt that the Sioux and Cheyenne suffered serious casualties in the Hayfield and Wagon Box fights.

Desiring a better weapon, the Army convened a board in 1872 to examine and test existing weapons. After the board had examined over a hundred weapons the Army adopted the single-shot Model 1873 Springfield breechloader. This fired a center-fire .45-caliber cartridge, the caliber that the Ordnance Department selected as most desirable for all rifles, carbines, and pistols. The 1889 model of this gun, which embodied its final modifications, was the last of the Army's single-shot, large-caliber, black-powder rifles and the principal shoulder arm of the National Guard as late as 1898.

During the battle at Little Bighorn in 1876, the 7th Cavalry troopers under George Custer were armed with the Springfield trapdoor carbine Model 1873 and the Colt Single Action Army revolver Model 1873. Selection of the weapons was the result of much trial and error, plus official testing during 1871-1873. The Ordnance Department staged field trials of 89 rifles and carbines, which included entries from Peabody, Spencer, Freeman, Elliot, and Mauser. There were four primary contenders: the Ward-Burton bolt-action rifle; the Remington rolling-block; the "trapdoor" Springfield; and the Sharps, with its vertically sliding breechblock. The Springfield was the winner. Although repeating rifles such as the Spencer, Winchester, and Henry had been available, the Ordnance Department decided to use a single-shot system.

The guns issued to Custer's men had been tested for defective cartridges, endurance, accuracy, rapidity of fire, firing with excessive charges, and effects of dust and rust. The full-length trapdoor Springfield could hurl a slug more than 1,000 yards and, with proper training, could be fired with accuracy 12 to 15 times per minute. The Model 1873 trapdoor carried by the 7th Cavalry was a carbine that weighed 7 pounds and had an overall length of 41 inches. It used a .45-55 caliber copper-cased cartridge, a 405-grain bullet and a charge of 55 grains of black powder. The best effective range for this carbine was somewhat less than 300 yards, but significant hits still could be scored out to 600 yards. The Single Action Army revolver was issued with a barrel of 7.5 inches. Each trooper had 24 rounds for his Colt handgun. A single disadvantage of the revolver was that there was no repeating rifle available at the time of the same caliber that was capable of sharing cartridge ammunition with it.

One of the most critical things to the operating efficiency of many lever action rifles was the over all length of the cartridge. Winchester lever action rifles were designed to operate optimally with a cartridge length of 1.600 inches. Winchester's repeating carrier block captures a round from the magazine, operates magazine tube, and elevates it to the firing chamber. However before the carrier can elevate the captured round upwards, it must also "shear" the next round in the magazine (leaving it slightly hanging out into the carrier) to wait its turn. When a given cartridge is too short, part of the next cartridge in line will come back even further into the carrier and cause the action to lock up, run very rough, or barely operate. This is seldom an issue with large calibers like the .45 Long Colt, .44-40, or 38-40, or the problem may go un-noticed until speed of loading becomes a factor. However, using .38 specials can sometimes pose problems.

Many Action Shooters use the .38 Special for the convenience of having the same ammunition for both handgun and rifle. Most modern lever-action rifles feed .38 specials with an overall length of 1.550 inches (39 mm). However, any 1873 must be fed a cartridge with a minimum length of 1.450 inches. This will allow the rifle to operate more smoothly and more reliably with a full magazine. Many individuals will use .357-magnum brass (case lengths: 1.290 v 1.155) when reloading their .38 special rounds. This allows them to achieve a longer length without seating the bullets further out of the case. The latter solution can be used, however, as the bullets do not need to be crimped in the crimp groove. Another cartridge requirement for 1873 Winchesters is a flat point on the bullet's nose. The 1873s dislike round noses. Without the flat point on the end of the cartridge (especially in the .38 special) the bullets will zigzag themselves in the magazine tube. This usually prevents the magazine from being fully loaded, and may cause the rifle to jam. Lever action rifles of all types will also not feed wad cutters reliably. The rim on the edge of the bullet acts as a hangnail when the round is entering the chamber. A minimum cartridge length of 1.450 inches is highly recommended (the longer the better: 1.475 inches or greater). Most factory .38 cartridges were too short to work optimally in 1873s because the specials were primarily designed for revolvers.

Almost as soon as Colt began shipping the SAA to the US Army in 1873, the company released them also for sale to civilians manufactured in .44-40 Winchester instead of .45 Colt and in three common barrel lengths (4.75, 5.5, 7.5 inches). The six-shooter was reliable, comparatively lightweight (2.3 pounds), and was almost impossible to destroy if given minimal care. This revolver and the Winchester Model 1873 or the Winchester Model 1892 lever action rifles in .44-40 WCF caliber were one of the most common combinations carried by civilians in "the Old West."

In most of his films, actor John Wayne carried a Colt 1896 Single Action Army pistol with butterscotch-colored single-screw grips and a 4.75-inch barrel – a model widely know as the Peacemaker. General George S. Patton Jr. famously carried of pair of Colt Single Action Armies with engraved ivory grips during World War II. A remarkable variant of the SAA was the so-called Buntline Special with its 12-inch barrel made famous in the 1950s by the television series "Wyatt Earp" starring Hugh O'Brian in the title role. In 1876, Dime Novel author Edward Zane Carroll Judson (a.k.a. Ned Buntline) had included the weapon in his stories about Earp and four other Dodge City lawmen Bat Masterson, Bill Tilghman, Charlie Bassett, and Neal Brown. There is no conclusive proof that Earp ever possessed such a weapon. Nevertheless, a letter of the period exists confirming that Buntline ordered the specially made pistols to be presented to Earp and other famous lawmen of the day in recognition for their exploits, and in appreciation for giving him inspiration for his western stories. Thirty-one such long barreled revolvers (10 to 16 inches) were actually produced between 1876 and 1884. They required a holster with an extended drop necessary for the long barrel to clear leather. Between 1957 and 1975, *Earpmania* caused Colt to produce more than 4,000 of these weapons. In 1880, a $20 gold piece (1 ounce) would buy a nice Colt revolver. In 2016, that same $20 gold piece (1 ounce) will still buy a nice Colt revolver. This may help to prove that guns are worth their weight in gold.[61]

12. Holsters

The western gun holster, a true and original art form, has had a long and colorful history. The common use of holsters mounted on a belt can be traced back to the decades before the Civil War and continued through the frontier period of the American west. Civilian style holsters were developed for the hip and shoulder, but many revolvers were marketed as pocket models. Some cavalrymen supplied themselves with several pistols: two in the pommel holsters on the saddle, one in the standard military waist belt holster, and one or more shoved in their waistband usually with a lanyard around their neck. The real Wyatt Earp usually slipped his pistols into his coat pockets, and Wild Bill Hickok shoved them into a sash wrapped around his waist with the butt ends facing forward.

Holsters were made to draw from the right hand, from the left, or across the body. As revolver advancements were made and they became more manageable, saddle makers designed a more accessible and efficient hip holster. William S. Hart, the first western superstar of the silent era, wore a comparatively plain (but authentic) gun rig. Significant improvements in western holsters peaked during the heyday of the 1940s and 1950s western film and television era.

After the turn of the 20th century, western lawmen, especially the Texas Rangers and US Border Patrol, contributed many alternative ideas to holster and saddle makers. By 1939, the Western film was falling out of favor, but *Stagecoach* with its seven Academy Awards helped reinvent the genre. Ironically, the star of the film, John Wayne never wears a gun holster. Filmmakers of the 1940s and 50s took great liberties with holster designs worn by their heroes and outlaws.

The gun belt design, known as the Ranger Belt, was adopted from an overlapping cinching technique used in horse tack that allows a strap to be tightened without pinching the horse's hair in the buckle. The Texas Rangers had adapted this belting technique into the design of a ranger holster in the 1840s, when they began using the heavy Colt Walker six-shooters (4.4 pounds), which required wider belts to support them. The technique eliminated the need for heavy belt buckles. The gun's heft made impractical the common practice of stuffing a pistol into the waistband of the bearer's pants, or into a cloth sash tied around the waist or hips. Colt introduced the roughly half-pound lighter Dragoon Model revolver in 1845.

Hollywood favored the Colt Peacemaker Model Single Action Army .45 caliber revolver for its actors. The six-shooter was reliable when used with full load BP blank cartridges, was visually intimidating on screen, comparatively lightweight (2.3 pounds), and was almost impossible to destroy if given minimal care. The SAA came in three different barrel lengths between 4.75 inches and 7.5 inches. Almost as soon as Colt began shipping .45s to the US Army in 1873, they released them also for sale to civilians. Records on the SAA Revolver are a Who's Who of action-oriented Americans of the late 19th and early 20th centuries including Buffalo Bill Cody, Theodore Roosevelt, Judge Roy Bean, Pat Garrett, General George Patton, and dozens of screen and TV stars. The Colt SAA revolver is famously known as "The Gun That Won the West." Although single action (it needs to be cocked before it is fired), it is possible to fire the SAA rapidly and with some precision by holding down the trigger and "fanning" the hammer with the other hand in Hollywood fashion. Of all Western-style handguns it is the most legendary and arguably the most esthetically pleasing. A single disadvantage of the gun was that there was no lever action rifle available of the same caliber that was capable of sharing ammunition with it.[62]

The first true western style holster was the "California pattern." These open-topped holsters were slender in profile and had a deep form-fitting body that gripped the revolver and sewn in toe plugs to keep debris out and help secure the gun. The holster was mounted on a belt by a leather loop sewn on the back. By 1876, the form-fitted "California Pattern," had been in vogue for a few decades, but the arrival of the self-contained metallic cartridge inspired a new breed of gun leather, the so-called "Mexican Loop" holster. Since the small belt loops on the backs of the slim-lined "California Pattern" were designed for the percussion age, Westerners quickly discovered a new type of holster that could fit over the bulkier, and often wider, cartridge-laden gun belts. The California-style bucket with a narrow loop on the holster's back side allowed for too much play, and it also caused the holstered pistol to hang loosely to the side, flopping around uncomfortably when the wearer was active, such as when riding horseback. The Mexican loop arrangement differed in that it consisted of a single piece of leather that formed the scabbard, backing and retaining loops on the holster body. This design created both a wide upper loop through which the cartridge belt could pass, securing the holster more firmly in place, while the skirt loops kept the pouch portion from riding up when the person drew his weapon. By the time of the introduction of the Mexican Loop holster, the trend in gun leather adornment had already shifted from the heavily carved floral motifs to simpler, border-stamped designs. The style readily lent itself to the newer "Buscadero" gun belts, in which the holster hung from a slot in the cartridge belt, rather than worn slipped over it. Like the 10-gallon hat, six-gun and silver-mounted spurs, the Mexican Loop holster—with all of its silver screen flamboyance—was assured a permanent place among the Westerner's classic gear.

Many B-Western movies used original surplus civil war guns, uniforms and buckles in their production sometimes repurposing carbine sling buckles on gun belts and firing blank rounds through genuine weapons from the Civil War. In 1932, future mega-star John Wayne appeared in a minor role in *Texas Cyclone* starring Tim Mc Coy, the latter properly festooned in a hand tool double holster with a large buckle. In 1936, Wayne wore a 2-inch square plate buckle in his role in the *Oregon Trail*. This is believed to be a lost film with no known prints remaining. In 2013, a collector found forty still photographs from the film. In 1948, Wayne, Henry Fonda and all the other major actors playing soldiers in *Fort Apache* wore original eagle buckles and rear facing flap holsters repurposed from Civil War surplus. The film was the first of the director John Ford's cavalry trilogy all starring Wayne. In these films, Wayne used a 3-inch long, 2-inch tall original Civil War buckle from his personal collection on a simple gun rig that would appear again in *El Dorado* (1966), *True Grit* (1969), and *Rooster Cogburn* (1975). He often carried the same Ivory handled Colt Single Action Army revolver with 4.75 inch barrel, referred to as a "Quick-Draw" or "Civilian" model high on his hip on a simple unadorned leather rig. This was often used to emphasize his personal and iconic rolling gait when walking.

The Buscadero was originally designed for Texas lawmen and Hollywood cowboys in the 1920's. To those who grew up in the TV cowboy era of Roy Rodgers, the Lone Ranger, and Hopalong Cassidy, the gun belt and dual bucket rig was set low on the hips and angled slightly forward for a faster draw. During the 1950s, the "Fast Draw" rig used a specially contoured Buscadero cartridge belt that placed the slotted holster tab even lower on the hip. Other film and TV stars using this style included such greats as Tex Ritter, Duncan Renaldo (the Cisco Kid), Gene Autry, Lash LeRue, William Boyd (Hopalong), and Clayton Moore (the Lone Ranger). These dual bucket rigs often had silver engraved ranger buckles, silver conchos, and leather carvings. These western stars wore custom-made, hand-tooled outfits that were edge laced and sported custom buckles and adornments usually in silver in order to personalize them. William Boyd wore the same holster from his second Hoppy movie, *The Eagle's Brood* made in 1935, until he retired from TV in the early 1950s. Boyd made 66 motion pictures before his television series began in 1948.

A social conscience struck Hollywood in the 1950s. Post-World War II Hollywood put the aggressive two-gun rig aside to be replaced by the simple and generally unadorned single bucket Buscadero. A leader among the counter-Westerns produced at this time was the award-winning movie *High Noon* (1952) starring Gary Cooper. As the forsaken Sheriff Will Kane, Cooper encounters young boys enacting a shoot-out with fingers and sticks. During the play-acting, one youngster shouts out: "Bang, bang, you're dead, Kane." Ethical quandaries drive *High Noon*, as the traditional notions of heroism and civic loyalty being permanent qualities are seemingly discarded. On its release the film was hailed as a masterpiece by the liberal elites. But film historians and theorists have also reviled it almost from the beginning as "pretentious social realism and the death of the Western." Herein they were largely in error. [63]

Unornamented and functional holsters later became the new gun rig of choice in most television and movie westerns thereafter and are still being used today. The Buscadero style holster was no more authentic or historically popular than other rigs, but it was used by almost every TV series for the next 30 years. *Gunsmoke, Bonanza, Maverick, Cheyenne, Sugarfoot, Wyatt Earp, The Lawman,* and *Colt .45* are just a few of the classic TV shows that used it. These shows and many movie companies hired gun expert Arvo Ojala to be their gun coach and technical advisor. It was his influence, not history, which drove its adoption. Topping the list as instantly recognizable is the Black Single Holster adorned with the silver Knight Chess Piece, made famous in the TV show *Have Gun Will Travel*. In the series *Gunsmoke*, which ran for 20 seasons from 1955 to 1975 and stands as the longest-running prime time, live-action drama in TV history, the main character Marshal Matt Dillon (James Arness) wore an unadorned holster for 635 episodes. The holster figured prominently in the opening credits for many years. Ojala was also one of the unnamed men shot by Arness in the several iterations of the opening sequence of the long-running television series.

The single bucket rig worn by star Lorne Greene, who played Ben Cartwright the family patriarch on second place *Bonanza*, represented the standard Hollywood fast draw Buscadero style of the period. From the fourth season on, the Cartwright's and nearly every other recurring character on the show wore the same clothing and accoutrements and rode the same horses in almost every episode. Greene's gun outfit was unusual for its spectacular carving and two-tone leather design as well as total lack of any bullet loops or large buckles on the gun belt. *Bonanza* was considered an atypical western for its time, but the story by David Dortort was originally set before the Civil War (1861) when cartridge handguns were rare and ended in its fourteenth season (1959-1973) set in 1867.

Nonetheless, the socially conscious Cartwright's seldom ran out of ammunition because they rarely resorted to gunfights.

About this time, Italian director Sergio Leone and actor Clint Eastwood, who starred in *Rawhide* on TV (1959-1965), helped to bring a more authentic and violent revisionism to the American western. Leone's films, although made mostly in Spain, paid tribute to traditional American westerns, but significantly departed from them in storyline, plot, characterization, and mood. A less decorative rig also without large buckles became popular in movies such as *The Good, Bad, and the Ugly* (1966) and many of the so-called classic Spaghetti Westerns with Clint Eastwood, Eli Wallach, or Lee Van Cleef. In one scene Wallach enters a gunfight with his pistol hanging from a lanyard about his neck. The holster used by Eastwood was sometimes called the "Walk and Draw" and used a leather-covered, metal plate over or behind the gun belt to help anchor it. The films also did much to popularize the Mexican poncho worn by Eastwood as the "Man With No Name." The poncho was Eastwood's own idea for the characterization, but it totally covered the holster and belt buckle. This forced the character to flip the corner over his shoulder as the gun action approached adding anticipation to the scene.

In 1973, Eastwood directed his first revisionist western, *High Plains Drifter*, in which he also starred, and then *The Outlaw Josey Wales* (1976), *Unforgiven* (1992), and others. These films contained both moral and supernatural themes. The brutally unembellished *Unforgiven* won three Academy Awards including Best Picture and Best Director. Peculiar to *Pale Rider*, Eastwood, who directed the film in 1985, chose to spend a good deal of screen time changing cylinders in his pistols even though the story takes place sometime in the 1870s or early 1880s when cartridge revolvers were available. The character called Preacher (Eastwood) carries an out-of-date Remington 1858 New Army with a cartridge conversion as his sidearm in the film, and carries several pre-loaded cylinders to use like a modern speed loader. He also uses a Remington 1858 Pocket .31 caliber as a backup, carrying it stuck into his belt.

The revisionist era in Western movies introduced new screen heroes like Willey Nelson, Kris Kristofferson, Kenny Rogers, Sam Elliot, Tom Selleck, and the Caradine (Keith, David, and Robert), Keach (Stacey and James), and Quaid (Randy and Dennis) brothers. It also made use of trumpets and whaling harmonicas in the background music. Cowpokes became dirtier, often black coated and ruthless, and more gray bearded and older than those of earlier decades. Gone were the fancy gun rigs, clean-shaven faces, and fringed jackets; and range-bred cowponies were replaced on the screen by high-stepping Spanish Paso Fino stock. All Pasos share their heritage with the Peruvian Paso, the American Mustangs, and other descendants of Colonial Spanish Horses.

Finally, in *Quigley Down Under* (1990), actor Tom Selleck as Matthew Quigley is hired as a sharpshooter by an Australian landowner Elliot Marston (played by Alan Rickman) who is fascinated by Old West gunfighting. Quigley, an expert with a sharps rifle, is lured to Australia to exterminate Aborigines. Quigley is repulsed by the idea, and several times states he has no use for handguns. Captured by Marston, who has noticed that Quigley only ever carries a rifle, the Australian decides to give him a lesson in the "quick-draw" style of gunfighting. Quigley is given a pistol, thrust into his waistband. As the two face off, Marston makes the first move drawing from his fast draw Buscadero, but is beaten by Quigley, who shoots Marston and his two remaining men. As Marston lies dying, Quigley tells him, "Said I never had much use for one [a handgun]; never said

I didn't know how to use it." Other elements in the film provide points of interest - the use of the Aborigine characters, for example, in roles usually reserved for Native Americans or African Americans in Hollywood Westerns. [64]

Nonetheless, a new generation of moviegoers, now in their teens, has grown up never having seen a shoot-um-up Western in a movie theater. Cowboy movies have become too genteel, maybe, or the violence of the Old West followed too strict an ethical code instead of being mindless like real-life gang drive-bys and terror shootings with automatic weapons. Cowboys today wear enormous belt buckles, polyester shirts and silk scarves, carry cell phones, ride mechanical bulls, and drink lite beer instead of Red Eye.

13. Clothing and Accoutrements

Spurs and spur straps

Horsemen have used spurs regularly since medieval times although the first example of spurs found have been dated to around 700 BC. The spur came into prominence during the medieval times of feudal lords and knights. For centuries mounted soldiers wore spurs as a status symbol and to help control their horses. By the 16th century spurs had found their way to America with the Spanish conquistadors. The Spanish vaqueros used them and were extremely proud of their horsemanship. Many employed a type of spur with sharp pointed rowels that could severally injure a horse if misused. Eventually many cowboys, ranchers, and mounted soldiers adopted the use of the spur. Leather spur straps came in several styles, and the designs ranged from plain and utilitarian to the highly ornate and fashionable, with or without conchos or studs.

James Butler "Wild Bill" Hickok was one of that peculiar class of Old West personalities known as gamblers and gunmen. Hickok was a lawman in Kansas and Nebraska. Just 30 years of age, he was shot in the back by Crooked Nose Jack McCall after a poker dispute in 1876.

Chaps

The concept of leather chaps was also introduced by the Spanish to protect their legs from cactus, brush, and thorns. They called these "Chaparehos" which loosely translated as leather breeches or "legs of iron." The first chaps were large pieces of cowhide attached to the saddle as fenders wrapping around the legs. Later designs hung from a belt around the waist and went down the leg to just below the knee. Rawhide thongs held the chaps to the leg. Early Texans designed a heavy buckskin breech that fully encircled the leg and often had fringe. Western leather makers generally made three types of chaps to accommodate the various general types of conditions in which they were used.

The three common types were termed Shotgun, Bat Wing, and Woolies. Shotgun chaps were seamless leather pants with a shape that reminded one of a double-barreled shotgun. This style was popular from the 1870s through the 1890s but their skin-tight cut and design (while fashionable) was hard to put on or take off while wearing a pair of boots and spurs. Bat Wing chaps appeared in the early 1900s and gained immediate acceptance because they had snap fasteners that allowed them to go on and come off easily. They were easy to decorate and could be made extremely ornate. Woolies became popular in the late 1800s on the northern plains, especially during cold and wet weather. These chaps were made from hides with the hair left on. They were made in a wide variety of local furs including bear and buffalo, but the most prized were of Angora goat fur. These chaps were a favorite of Wild West show performers who loved the look.

Commonly used in the southwest, so-called Chinks were half-length chaps that attached at the waist and ended just below the knee, usually with a very long fringe at the bottom and along the sides. This feature made them appear much longer than they were. The cut was a hybrid of the Bat Wing and Shotgun, and each leg had two fasteners located high up on the thigh. These were cooler to wear than a full length chap, and they were adopted by southwestern cowboys when not riding through tough terrain.

Wrist cuffs

Wrist cuffs first appeared in photographs and saddle catalogs in the 1890s and may have derived from the military style leather gauntlets that were also worn by cowboys. The first cuffs tied around the wrist with laces. They had two functions. One was to protect the cuffs of the shirt from wear — store-bought shirts being fairly expensive. The second function of the cuff was to protect the wrist from the kicking hooves when branding cattle. They eventually became a traditional cowboy accessory and fashion statement featuring carved or stamped designs and decorated with spots and conchos.

A young man was all decked out in Old West fashion for this studio photograph.

The Duster

The original dusters were full-length, light-colored canvas or linen coats worn by horsemen to protect their clothing from trail dust. These dusters were typically slit up the back to the hip for ease of wear on horseback and were the recommended in place of a "uniform" for the early Texas Rangers. Dusters intended for riding may have features such as a buttonable rear slit and leg straps to hold the flaps in place. For better protection against rain, dusters were often made from oilcloth and later from waxed cotton.

A duster worn by actor Jack Elam.

They figured little in Western films until Sergio Leone re-introduced them in his movies *The Good, the Bad, and the Ugly* (1966) and *Once Upon a Time in the West* (1968). *The Great Northfield Minnesota Raid*, a 1972 Western film concerning the James-Younger Gang featured these garments. Dusters are now a standard item of western wear among Old West reenactors and Cowboy Action Shooters.

Men's attire

In his handbook of etiquette from the period, Arthur Martine remarks, "There are four kinds of coats which a man must have: a business coat, a frock-coat, a dress-coat, and an over-coat. A well dressed man may do well with four of the first, and one each of the others per annum. An economical man can get along with less." Nonetheless, Martine's idea of "getting along" was nowhere near reality. Just as the average woman did not have a specialized outfit for every task of the day, most men did not enjoy the wardrobe depth detailed by Martine. Like women's clothing, men's clothing in practical application tended to fall into formal and informal, summer and winter. New clothes would be considered "best" dress until they became worn, and they would then be relegated to work status. (Martine, 1866, 43)

William Barclay "Bat" Masterson was photographed in 1879 in a simple cloth coat and fashionable Derby. Masterson moved to Denver and established himself as a leading "sporting man," or gambler. He was briefly a lawman in Dodge City and several other towns. The "Wild West" phase of Masterson's life was essentially over by the mid 1880s when he was still in his early thirties. He made a living as a newspaper columnist.

Many men wore a simple cloth jacket extending just below the hip with a straight back and no seam at the waist widely known as a sack coat. This could be worn with a matching set of trousers and waistcoat (vest) for a "better dressed" but less formal look. The jacket usually had two capacious side pockets, and sometimes an elongated inside breast pocket sometimes called a "poacher's" pocket. Vests or waistcoats could be made of the same fabric as the jacket, or they could be of contrasting, finer, or dressier fabrics such as silk taffetas, embossed silks, or brocades. Patterns ranged from tone-on-tone to stripes, checks, and paisleys. Waistcoat watch pockets were common.

The woolen sack coat was the precursor to the donkey jacket worn from the mid Victorian era onwards by workers and soldiers. A shirt, vest, and trousers would be the very least in which a man would allow himself to be seen. A man appearing with anything less was considered to be in a state of undress. Even laborers and farmers would not allow themselves to go with less. It was the basest menial or workman who would not be so attired unless pressed by circumstances, such as the blacksmith, who would wear a heavy leather apron, which covered him above the waist.

Dress shirts were made of white cotton. Longer than the modern shirt, they were pullovers that buttoned from the mid-chest to the neck. Small vertical tucks commonly decorated either side of the buttons, but this became less favored as the century progressed. Some shirts had neckbands and detachable collars. For formal day wear, the collar was upright with a gap between the points, which just touched the jaw, allowing for freer movement of the head and neck than had been the style earlier in the century. For informal occasions, men wore either a shallow single collar with sloping points meeting at the center and forming a small inverted "V" opening, or a shallow double collar similar to the modern collar.

Work shirts were made in a variety of colors and checks and could be made from cotton or linen. However, as machine made cotton became less costly most persons moved away from linen. Fine linen thread is not elastic, and therefore it is difficult to machine weave without breaking threads. Thus linen became considerably more expensive to manufacture than cotton. The survival on the frontier of the coarse linen shirt (homespun) was due to the fact that the cloth could be spun and woven by hand.

Cravats, which more closely resemble the earlier neck stock than the modern tie, were worn around the neck. The term "necktie" was just coming into use. The cravat might have been tied in a flat, broad bow with the ends extending across the top of the waistcoat or secured with a pin. Basically, however, it was a band of fabric passed around the neck and tied in either a bow or a knot with wide hanging ends. Silk was the fabric of choice, and it was one area where a man might be able to display his good taste even if his purse prohibited further extravagances. The decade began with a preference for light-colored cravats, occasionally decorated with embroidery or other fancy work. As the century progressed, however, darker colors became more prominent. Striped, plaid, and dotted cravats (a la Clark Gable in his first iconic appearance in the 1939 film *Gone With the Wind*) were also worn, but with less regularity. Even laborers would simulate the look, although they may only have been able to knot a cotton kerchief around their neck. Ladies' magazines of the period offered patterns for woolen and cotton knitted cravats. A pattern for a striped tie done in brioche knitting in Peterson's ended with, "We recommend this for a present for the holidays." (Shep, 1987, 345)

Suits were either loose fitting, almost baggy, or very formal with knee-length frock coats. The fuller suit seems to have been favored by the average man, perhaps because it was more comfortable or needed less skilled tailoring. Shorter than a frock coat, the town coat was appropriate for work, but the formal suit appears to have been the "look" to which men of power aspired. Lapels sported a more modern single notch than earlier in the century. Frock coats sometimes had velvet collars and cuff link style buttoning.

Many work trousers had buttoned or full fall fronts, while dress trousers had "French flys," which concealed the buttons. Most trousers today are held up through the assistance of a belt that is passed through the belt loops on the waistband. Until the early 1900s, however, American men did not generally wear belts on their trousers at all. Most men, civilian and military, held their high-waisted pants up with braces, a non-elastic form of suspenders, not belts. Belts became more popular as fashion accessories as the tops of trousers moved from just under the ribs toward the more natural waist in the early 20th century. Braces were more comfortable than belt cinching. Unfortunately, they were also prone to sudden catastrophic failure as one or more buttons became unfixed.

Levi Strauss, noted for his durable work pants, opened his dry goods wholesale business as Levi Strauss & Co. in San Francisco in 1853 and imported fine dry goods—clothing, bedding, combs, purses, and handkerchiefs—from his brothers in New York.

Jacob Davis, a tailor from Reno, Nevada partnered with Strauss in 1871 to patent and sell clothing reinforced with copper rivets. The rivets reinforced the points of stress, such as pocket corners and at the bottom of the button fly, which miners and laborers had found to fail prematurely. Often the term "jeans" refers to a particular style of pants, called "blue jeans," but the men experimented with different fabrics. An early attempt was tried with brown cotton duck. Jeans are typically made from denim (canvass twill) or dungaree cloth. Dungaree is often conflated with denim. The two fabrics are colored in different ways, dungaree traditionally being woven from pre-colored yarn, while denim was made from uncolored yarn and only colored after weaving. It was found that only a few grams of blue indigo dye were required for each pair. Eliza Lucas Pinckney had introduced wide scale indigo production into colonial South Carolina, where it became the colony's second-most important cash crop (after rice) in the 1740s.

Wool was the fabric of choice for many clothing items, with linen being popular during the summer. Wool is warm and sturdy, holds its color, and does not loose its thermal qualities when wetted. Wool can absorb almost one-third of its own weight in water. Wool has a very low propensity to burn, while linen burns quickly. It is usually specified for garments for firefighters, soldiers, and others in occupations where they are exposed to the likelihood of fire. A homespun combination of wool and linen known as linsey-woolsey combined light weight with some protection against fire.

Farmers and laborers seem to favor moisture-resistant and durable tweeds and other sturdy woolens. Color effects in the cloth were obtained by mixing dyed yarns. Generally, solids dominated, with browns and grays most common. Black was the choice of professionals, who also preferred fine woolen broadcloth, serge, and twill. These fabrics often had a certain amount of silk woven in to give them a finer finish and lighter weight. Martine advises gentlemen:

> If a gentleman is able to dress expensively it is very well for him to do so, but if he is not able to wear ten-dollar broadcloth, he may comfort himself with the reflection that cloth, which costs but five dollars a yard will look quite as well when made into a well-fitting coat. With this suit, and well-made shoes, clean gloves, a white pocket-handkerchief, and an easy and graceful deportment withal, he may pass muster as a gentleman. (Martine, 1866, 49)

Hat styles varied. A form of peaked cap, also known as an immigrant's cap, mechanic's cap, or miner's cap, had a soft fabric crown, a band, and a peak or a visor. The steeply angled peak or visor was short, historically made of cloth or polished Japanned leather. The stovepipe hat favored by Abraham Lincoln also came in a shorter and longer-lived version. Many gentlemen favored what has come to be called the plantation hat. This is a low-crowned, stylish hat with a substantial, but not overstated, brim. The design of the plantation hat may have been brought back from Panama, where travelers had seen a similar hat while crossing the Isthmus to the gold fields of California. A wide and flat brimmed neutral color hat, the Stetson Boss of the Plains was immediately popular in the American Southwest. The Stetson Cowboy hat was an essential part of a drover's gear. The pork pie hat had a narrower brim and a flat top with a circular indent. It was popular from 1830 through the Civil War. The term *fedora* was in use as early as 1891. Its popularity soared, and eventually it eclipsed the similar-looking homburg characterized by a single dent running down the center of the crown. Many people wore flat-topped straw hats in summer. Rural men often wore wide-brimmed high-crowned hats, which offered less in fashion but more in protection from the elements. The derby, or bowler hat was designed in 1849 in London. The bowler was among the most popular hats in the American West, and has been called "the hat that won the West." More bowlers are seen in Western photo-portraits from the 1870s and 1880s than Stetsons. (Lucius Beebe)

Male jewelry was not as ostentatious as it had been in earlier periods. Rings of all types were popular. They took the form of signet rings, seal rings, mourning rings, and commemorative rings. Smaller neckties made the tiepin unnecessary in most cases. The longer coats of the sixties made the watch chain, which hung below a short waistcoat, impractical. The watch chain was now displayed from the waistcoat pocket to a button at mid-chest. In inclement weather, men often carried large black umbrellas.

Braces or suspenders buttoned on to the trousers by means of leather tabs. It was quite the fashion for women to crochet braces or work them in Berlin woolwork. Ladies' magazines featured patterns for this work, but makers were cautioned, "This crochet should not be done too tightly, as a little elasticity is desirable." (Shep, 290; Weaver) Elastic, made from natural rubber, had been invented by this time, but its only apparel application was in wide panels in shoes. Men unfortunate enough to have no braces made by an attentive woman may have sported those made of plain or striped linen.

Underwear required two pieces. The undershirt was a long-sleeved pullover that buttoned to mid-chest. The drawers extended down to the ankle and had button fronts. They could be made of silk stockinette, cotton, or linen. One-piece union suits, with or without the "trap door" in the rear, were not developed until the 1890s.

When it came to lounging in the privacy of one's home, gentlemen had several specialized items of attire. Lounging or smoking caps were elaborate items made of rich fabrics and adorned with embroidery, beadwork, or braid. They generally came in three basic styles: the round pillbox style, the fitted six-panel cap, and the teardrop-shaped Scotch style. The first two styles ended with a tassel on top. The last was finished with a narrow ribbon at the back of the cap at the point. Ladies' magazines also carried patterns for making and decorating these caps. Peterson's suggests that a hand-made lounging cap "would make a very pretty Christmas, New Year's, or birthday gift for a gentleman." (Shep, 344; Weaver) In addition to slippers. which greatly resembled the woman's slipper for relaxed footwear at home, a man might have preferred the dressing, or lounging boot. *Peterson's* advises, "The Lounging Boot, will almost supersede the slipper, as many gentlemen catch cold by changing from a boot to a slipper, even in the house." These boots were made of fabric and were decorated with elaborate embroidery. (Shep, 275; Weaver)

Nightshirts were made of white cotton and extended to the ankle. They had long sleeves and small turned-down collars. The nightcap was a bag-shaped item with a tassel on top. Some were knit or crocheted, but these were going out of style. Over his nightshirt a gentleman may have worn a wrapper. This was a long, sack-style robe with plain sleeves, confined by a cord at the waist.

Men wore their hair parted naturally to the side or more rarely down the center for affect. Beards and moustaches were constantly in fashion. Before the Civil War, hair had been worn longer, sometimes to extraordinary length as with George Custer. After 1860, and until the end of the century, hair was generally shorter although some men like William Hickok and Bill Cody wore it very long. Facial hair was very stylish. Men sported beards of all styles, lengths, and degrees. Mustaches were equally in favor. Period photographs show a tremendous variety of styles. The names of most of these have become meaningless to modern observers. The term "sideburns," however, can be traced to General Ambrose Burnside, who sported distinctively bushy whiskers. The size and style of sideburns and beards varied greatly between individuals and over time.

Gentlemen used different kinds of waxes and oils to keep their hair in shape, including wood frames used at night to preserve the form of their moustaches. At the end of the century many turned to a clean-shaven face and short hair. Amongst all the products used to condition or fix the hair, the most popular was Macassar oil. Made with a mix of coconut oil, palm oil and oil from flowers called "ylang-ylang," Macassar oil was thought to strengthen the hair and promote hair growth. It was sometimes combined with blacking as a hair "dye." Due to the tendency for the oil to transfer from the user's hair to the back of his chair, the antimacassar was developed. This was a small cloth (crocheted, embroidered or mass-produced), placed over the back of a chair to protect the upholstery.

In 1939, actor John Wayne wore suspenders and a simple belt at the same time to hold up his trousers in *Stagecoach*, the movie that made him a star. He never wears a gun belt during the film, but the belt on his trousers was used to emphasize his thin waist and lanky countenance. Wayne first appears twirling and re-cocking his Winchester rifle in one hand, while holding his saddle in the other. He is standing in the middle of the desert wearing a paneled, placket-front buttoned shirt with a neckerchief, Stetson hat, and jeans with its pants legs rolled up outside of his boots – a look attempted by thousands of little boys thereafter.

The Stetson

In 1865, with $100, John B. Stetson rented a small room in Philadelphia; bought the tools and materials he needed; and began a hat company. Stetson had attempted to join the Union Army in the early 1860s, but due to poor health he was rejected. He joined a group headed west seeking their fortunes mining for gold, but one year of fruitless searching for gold was enough. He noted that everyone in the West wore some kind of hat. Weather and exposure made it necessary to cover the head. Trained by his father, a master hatter, John applied his skills and knowledge to a trade that at the time was not held in high regard.

Possibly suffering from an undiagnosed neurological disease brought on by excessive exposure to mercury, hatters were seen as unreliable, lazy, aloof, or even mentally unstable, hence the Mad Hatter from Lewis Carroll's *Alice's Adventures in Wonderland*. The manufacture of hats from fur entailed a process known as felting, in which the hair was cut from the pelt (usually that of wool or rabbit), washed and laid layer upon layer on a conical mould, and pressed and shrunk with steam or hot water. The washing operation was very important to the quality of the completed hat, as any little particles of dirt allowed to be rolled up inside the fiber, would produce a bumpy surface and dirty spots. The advantage of adding mercuric nitrate during felting was that it made the outer stiff hairs on the pelt soft and limp, and twisted and roughened them so that they packed together more easily. The psychotic symptoms of mercury poisoning had been described during the eighteenth century, when mercurial ointments were used in the treatment of syphilis.

With the Eastern hat market difficult, Stetson turned his attention to the West. He had made the right choice. Before the invention of the Stetson cowboy hat, drovers on the plains wore castoffs of previous lives and vocations. The common hat was made of wool felt. Men moving westward wore formal top hats and derbies, leftover remnants of Civil War headgear, tams, and sailor hats. A wide brim hat, much like the plantation hats of the Deep South or the straw Mexican sombrero, were common by those living in sunny climates.

The Hardee hat, also known as the Model 1858 Dress Hat, was the regulation dress hat for enlisted men in the Union Army during the Civil War. Confederate soldiers also wore the Hardee hat, but it was stiff and hot due to its dark color. The pillbox hat was probably the most widely used style in the South during the war. The wide-brimmed variant was the favorite. Pinning up the side or front of the brim was called slouching. The name "slouch hat," being fairly common among officers, refers to the fact that one side droops down as opposed to the other which is pinned against the side of the crown. The headgear was common among Confederate and Union troops in the Western Theater, although not always with its brim turned up at the side. Nineteenth century hat expert Bill Wickham notes that the Trans-Mississippi region and the West in general tended to lag behind in fashion trends, but slouch hats were more common in the western theaters of the war than elsewhere. (See Adolphus)

However, a wide and flat brimmed neutral color hat, the Stetson Boss of the Plains (his first model), was immediately popular in the American Southwest. Before the introduction of the Boss of the Plains, cavalry troopers wore hats in a similar style, but quickly adopted the Boss of the Plains as an unofficial standard. For years, however, Stetson worried about the waterproofing of his rabbit felt hats, and finally decided to make his hat of beaver felt. Because of the tighter weave most Stetsons were waterproof enough to be used as a bucket. Stetson featured advertising of a cowboy watering his horse with water carried in the crown, a scene repeated in many Hollywood movies.

Western hats offered by Stetson from 1870 to 1900 included the Boss of the Plains, Alaska, Columbia, Dakota, and Railroad styles. Texans were known for their preference for the "Ten Gallon" model. The term "ten-gallon" had nothing to do with the hat's size, but derives from the Spanish word *galón* (braid), indicating the ten braids used as a hatband. Early on, Stetson hats became associated with legends of the West, including Buffalo Bill Cody, Calamity Jane, and Annie Oakley. It is said that George Custer rode into the Battle of Little Big Horn wearing a Stetson although he was known to favor a Stetson straw hat rather than a fur felt one. Later on, Western movie cowboys were quick to adopt the Stetson being drawn to the largest, most flamboyant styles available for use in a visual medium. Tom Mix – Hollywood's first Cowboy star not only wore Stetson hats, he carried a dozen of them when traveling. He gave them to officials and dignitaries he met. Super star John Wayne christened the Stetson "The hat that won the West." Robert Baden-Powell later adopted the Campaign or Lemon Squeezer model of Stetson for use by the Boy Scouts. This is the same model associated with drill instructors, park rangers, the Royal Canadian Mounted Police, and Smokey the Bear.

The Stetson was the standard in hats, the essence of the spirit of the West and an icon of everyday American life. The Stetson Cowboy hat was an essential part of a drover's gear. Today's cowboy hat has remained basically unchanged in construction and design since the first one was created in 1865. By 1872, Stetson was also marketing his dress hats in his own catalog. As the twentieth century began, he had the world's largest hat factory with 25 buildings. The factory covered 9 acres of ground, employed 5400 people and was producing 3,000,000 hats annually. These were supplied to 10,000 retail merchants and 150 wholesale distributors. Roughly 1125 of the retail merchants were in foreign countries. Because of its authentic American heritage, Stetson remains as a part of its history.

14. Horses

Casting the right horse for a movie role is just as vital as casting the right leading man or lady. Like their human co-stars, equines must learn to play their part, sometimes through dozens of takes. Patience, good behavior, and good looks are the greatest virtues of a movie horse. [65]

John Wayne was responsible for a number of changes in *The Shootist* including having his last movie horse, Dollor written into the script. A dark chestnut sorrel with a very wide blaze and white stockings to the knee on the right front and both hind legs, Dollor had appeared in *The Undefeated*, *Rio Lobo*, *Chisum*, and *True Grit*. Another horse with similar markings, called "Dollar," appeared in *The Cowboys*, *The Train Robbers*, *Big Jake*, *Cahill - U.S. Marshall*, and *Rooster Cogburn*.

The early image of John Wayne riding a white horse through the Old West is a lasting one, but it wasn't just white horses that the actor used. The first white horse was "Duke, the Miracle Horse." The reason for the white horse was simple: the low budget studio wanted to use stock footage of another white horse, "Tarzan," who had appeared in Old West silent films with Ken Maynard. This tactic also forced Wayne to wear similar clothing. It also helps to explain the out-of-synchronization of hoof-beats in his early films.

Wayne may be the most popular cowboy movie star of all time, but he was reportedly not overly fond of horses, which he considered mere movie props. Nonetheless, he raised horses on his ranch in later years, and was known to ride in his free time; but he did not own his film mounts. In the film "El Dorado" Wayne rode an Appaloosa named "Cochise," which animal the actor did not like. The horse actually belonged to the film's director, Howard Hawks. Wayne's mounts were always big horses and throughout his film career he used several different regular mounts, including "Duke," "Starlight," "Banner," "Steel," "Alamo," "Dollar," "Beau," and "Dollor." In the dramatic fight at the conclusion of *True Grit*, Rooster's horse (clearly Dollor from his markings) is shot, trapping Rooster's leg under him as he goes down. "First time you ever give me reason to ... cuss you, Beau!" growls Wayne. The genuine Beau can be seen jumping the fence with Wayne in the final scene of *True Grit*. "You are too old and fat to be jumping horses," says Mattie (actress Kim Darby). "Well, come see a fat old man some time!" answers Wayne as he clears the fence. It was John Wayne, not a stuntman, who actually rode the horse over the fence.

15. Saddles

In the west the saddle was not only a tool that was used everyday but a symbol of stature. Many cowboys did not own their horses but if they had their own saddle they could get a job just about anywhere. An average custom rig from a western saddle maker in the 1870s could cost from $30 to $50. When a cowhand earned a dollar a day, this was a huge investment. Most cowboys considered their rig their most important possession and by taking excellent care of a well-made saddle it could last up to 20 years or more of daily use.

The American stock saddle evolved from the early Spanish military saddle used by the conquistadores. The Mexican vaquero's adapted the original saddle that had a heavy rigid tree, high fork and cantle, deep-dished seat and short stirrups. They made a few minor modifications and added a rounded leather skirt. In the late 1700s the Mexican "California" saddle had a fixed skirt and a more substantial rigging, which consisted of a cinch ring that hung down in line with the front fork and a horizontal strap that ran from the cinch to the back of the tree to secure the saddle. The strong high-peaked pommel of this saddle was ideal for taking a turn around a rope for holding an animal. These ultimately became the "classic cowboy saddle" of the late 1880s. More elaborate in design because of the Spanish/Mexican influence, they weren't designed to chase wild cattle.

The Texans then altered the latter design into the "Texas" saddle. They kept the wooden saddletree, horn, cantle, and stamped leather, but they modified the wooden horn into a short, thick post covered in leather. Texas saddles have low horns, slick forks, and double rigging. The skirt, in particular, was changed from a rounded shape to a plain square, and the stirrups were made out of wide steam-bent pieces of wood that were much stronger than the carved ones previously used. A second cinch was also added to firmly anchor the saddle when dealing with longhorn cattle, which were much more difficult than domesticated ones. In the 1870s they changed the horn again to a short metal one as the wooden ones often broke when dealing with wild cows. These rugged rigs were designed to chase wild cattle through heavy underbrush.

Different saddles were more popular in some areas than others. Many new designs and innovations came about with the input that saddlers received from their clientele, ranchers, and cowboys. With people moving into the west from the east there were many different styles of saddles seen. Georgia and the Carolinas had Plantation saddles, and the Morgan saddle came from the east. Mountain men, pioneers and early cowboys used the "Hope" saddle. The Hope has a full seat with extensive underskirts, fenders, and hooded stirrups. It has a wide front rigging and a decorative cap. Hope saddles were popular from the 1850s through the 1890s and recommended for use in the Confederacy during the second half of the Civil War. The Cheyenne saddle was distinguished by a fancy rolled cantle. The Montana saddle had large square skirts with wide fenders and exposed stirrup leathers. Pueblo saddles were larger than most, measuring up to 32 inches the fenders made the rig seem even wider. Developed by Gallup and Frazier in Pueblo, Colorado, this rig was quite beautiful and highly ornate. The wide skirt allowed for more decoration than normal. The saddle retained the double rigging and had a metal horn that was exposed. The metal horn was usually made of highly polished brass or nickel and was not practical for a serious cowboy work. The Oregon saddle was of a similar design to the California (a.k.a. Ranger) saddle but without all the ornamentation; and it has a swell fork made for working cattle on uneven terrain. Victor Mardin is said to have designed the swell fork around 1904. Before the swell fork the rider would have to wrap something around the pommel for a little more security on a rough mountain trails.

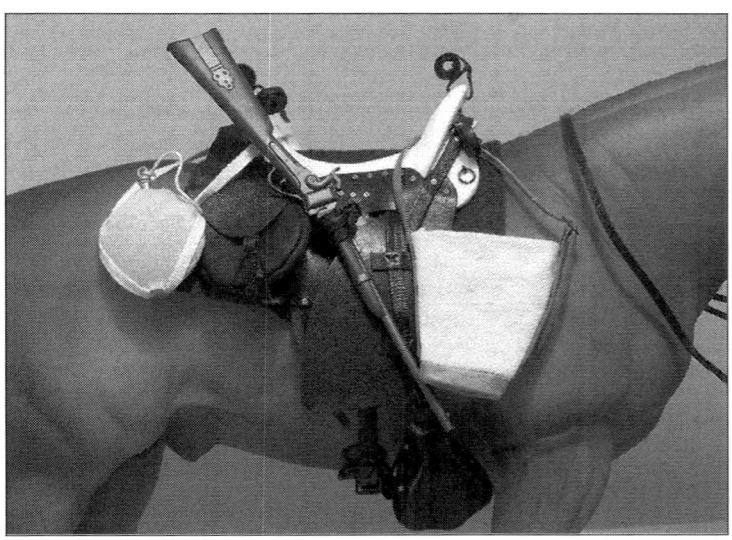

The photograph above shows a 1859 model McClellan Saddle on a well-turned-out mount. The rawhide seat was fitted with black leather skirts for protection of the legs, but many troopers removed them in consideration of the weight. Officers' models were often completely done in finished leather. The McClellan was easy on the horse's back, if not always on the rider's seat. The rawhide seat on the troopers' model had a tendency to crack when wet. These cracks with their raised edges could become quite uncomfortable for the rider.

The US Calvary (and many mounted state agencies) used the McClellan Calvary Saddle before and during the Civil War. It had an English-type tree with a higher pommel and cantle. The area the rider sits on is divided into two sections with a gap between the panels. The McClellan saddle was a riding saddle designed by George B. McClellan, a career Army officer in the U.S. Army, after his tour of Europe as the member of a military commission charged with studying the latest developments in mounted forces including field equipment. Based on his observations, McClellan proposed a design that was adopted by the Army in 1859. Dabney Maury, who was an instructor at West Point with McClellan, wrote: "He was a constant student of his profession. Having been instructed in the Classics and in French before he came to the Academy, he learned Spanish and German there, and before he was sent to Europe to study and report upon the cavalry service of the great military powers of the world, he had acquired sufficient knowledge of the Russian language to enable him to make a satisfactory and valuable report. The excellent saddles and horse equipage, ever since used in our service, were introduced by him from the Cossacks."[66]

Largely due to the exigencies of warfare, army horses were often used with great brutality. In addition to the trooper, his weapons and ammunition, they had to carry two saddlebags filled with extra clothing, a nose-bag filled with corn, a heavy leather halter, an iron picket-pin with a long picket rope, two extra horseshoes, a pair of blankets (one used as a saddle pad) and a rubber poncho, currycomb, brush and gun tools, the whole equipage weighing as much as 70 pounds over and above the weight of the rider, saddle, and harness. The McClellan saddle was a success largely because of its light weigh, rugged construction, and ability to distribute weight more evenly across the horse's back; and it continued in use in various forms until the US Army's last horse cavalry and horse artillery was dismounted during World War II.

16. Bridles

A bridle is a piece of equipment used to help direct a horse. It is most often composed of leather. The common practice of looping the reins on a hitch rack as seen in Hollywood films is actually a non-starter for most horsemen. A halter is used to lead or tie up an animal. Compared to halters, most bridles are made of thin leather, which will more easily break under pressure. Halters are often plain in design, and used as working equipment on a daily basis. Horse halters are sometimes confused with a bridle. Some users, including the military, have the animal wear a halter at all times, even when mounted, stalled, or turned out. The attached lead rope (or leather tether) is sometimes fitted as a loop around the mount's neck in the manner of the Royal Canadian Mounted Police.

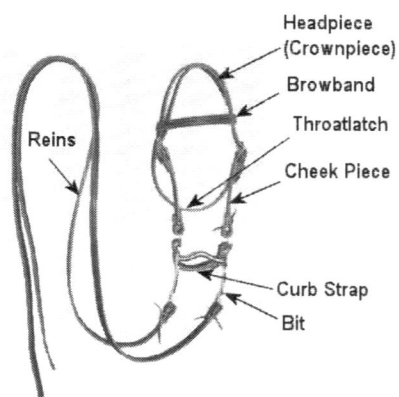

PARTS OF THE WESTERN BRIDLE

The bridle includes both the headstall that holds a metal bit that goes in the mouth of a horse, and the leather reins that are attached to the bit. A curb bit is a type of bit that uses lever action. It includes the Pelham bit and the Weymouth curb (a type of bridle that carries two bits) along with the traditional "curb bit" used mainly by Western riders. A Pelham bit functions similar to a double bridle acting on a single piece of metal, and like a double bridle it normally has a "double" set of reins: a set of curb reins and a set of snaffle reins – four in all. The historic Vaquero bit was a design with straight, highly decorated shanks and a mouthpiece that includes a straight bar, a narrow port with a cricket, and a "spoon," a flat, partly rounded plate affixed above the port, supported by braces on either side. Types of headgear for horses that exert control with a noseband rather than a bit are usually called hackamores though the term "bitless bridle" has become a popular colloquialism in recent years. The action and severity of the bit must correspond to the character and willingness of the horse for the activity that is planned.

A curb bit works on several parts of a horse's head and mouth. The bit mouthpiece acts on the bars, tongue and roof of the mouth. The shanks add leverage and place pressure on the poll via the crownpiece of the bridle, to the chin groove via the curb chain, and may act on the sides of the mouth and jaw. The longer the bit shank, the more powerful its potential effect on the horse. A high port (or metal arch in the bit) may act on the roof of the mouth as it touches. The US Cavalry offered curb bits with low, medium, and high ports so that the individual mount might be best managed in a manner best suited to its disposition.

Some western style curbs, particularly the Spade Bit, have both a straight bar mouthpiece and a high welded port, thus acting on the bars, tongue and palate. Curb bits can also be purchased with a variety of jointed mouthpieces some of which (like the twisted wire) can further increase severity. These bits, sometimes mistakenly called "cowboy snaffles" due to their popularity among western riders, are actually more harsh than a curb with a simple, solid, ported mouthpiece. In the wrong hands, such bits can be extremely severe, but on well-trained animals, they allow the accomplished rider to communicate with the horse with a simple touch of the fingertips to the reins. Modern western bits with moderately curved or angled shanks are sometimes called grazing bits, allegedly to allow the horse to graze while wearing a curb bit.

The reins of a bridle attach to the bit, below the attachment for the cheekpieces. The reins are the rider's link to the horse, and are seen on every bridle. Although dudes often have their reins knotted together so that they will not drop to the ground, true Western style reins are generally kept as two separate pieces. Closed reins, or loop reins, are either a single piece or buckle together at the ends. English riders usually use closed reins. Western riders in timed rodeo events use a single closed rein, as do those who use a romal, a rein style from the vaquero tradition that incorporates a closed rein with a long rawhide quirt at the end used to assist in moving cattle. A closed rein helps prevent the rider from dropping the reins. Reins are often laced, braided, or have stops worked into them to provide extra grip. When riding in the Western style, riders hold both reins in the left hand (if they are right-handed). This was so that they could hold a lariat or other needed tool in their right hand. This style was also used in the military where weapons such as swords or pistols were used right-handed.

Reins are used to give subtle commands or cues, also known as rein aids. Various commands may signal a turn, ask for a slower speed, request a halt or rein back. Rein aids are used along with leg aids, shifting of body weight, and sometimes voice commands. A neck rein is a type of *indirect* rein aid. The horse responds to a neck rein when it has learned that a light pressure of the right rein against its neck on that side means for the horse to turn left, and vice versa. A horse that has been well trained to neck rein becomes so responsive to the legs and seat of the accomplished rider that it is possible to take the bridle off completely — a move sometime seen in non-competitive exhibitions. Not all mounts will submit to neck rein training. A so-called cutting horse possesses an innate ability to anticipate or *read* a cow's intended moves, an ability commonly referred to as having *cow sense* or *cow smarts*. Cutting horses that are well trained and properly conditioned possess skills honed to respond instantaneously, matching a cow's every move, head to head, in order to contain it and separate it from the pack.

The crownpiece, or headstall of the bridle goes over the horse's head just behind the animal's ears, at the poll. It is the main strap that holds the remaining parts of the bridle in place. On most bridles, two cheekpieces attach to either side of the crownpiece and run down the side of the horse's face, along the cheekbone and attach to the bit rings. The throatlatch is usually part of the same piece of leather as the crownpiece. It runs from the horse's right ear, under the horse's throat, and attaches below the left ear. The main purpose of the throatlatch is to prevent the bridle from coming off over the horse's head, which can occur if the horse rubs its head on an object, or if the bit is low in the horse's mouth and tightened reins raise it up, loosening the cheeks. The crownpiece often runs through a browband. The browband runs from just under one ear of the horse, across the forehead, to just under the other ear. It prevents the bridle from sliding behind the poll onto the upper neck. The noseband encircles the nose of the horse. It is often used to keep the animal's mouth closed, or to attach other pieces or equipment.

Used for American-style western riding, the so-called Western bridle usually does not have a noseband. Many western bridles also lack browbands, sometimes replaced by one-ear designs (variations called split ear, shaped ear, and slip ear) where a small strap encircles one or both ears to provide extra security to keep the bridle in place. The bit goes into the horse's mouth, resting on the sensitive interdental space between the horse's teeth known as the "bars."

APPENDIX 1

When a powder charge is ignited, the granules don't all immediately ignite. The ignition has to propagate through the charge by leaping from one granule to another. A hot spray of salts ejected from burning granules ignites adjacent granules. Black powder of a particular grain size burns at essentially the same rate regardless of increasing pressure in the chamber or in the cartridge. BP burns at a rate dependent largely on the grain size and its surface area. FG is generally considered powder appropriate for canon, FFG for rifles, FFFG for handguns, and FFFFG for priming only. Therefore, the burn rate and pressure curve rise times for BP are generally independent of the pressure levels in the chamber or cartridge. Inappropriately fine-grained powder often caused cannons to burst before the projectile could move down the length of the barrel, due to the high initial spike in pressure. In the mid-19th century, measurements were made determining that the burning rate within a granule of black powder (or a tightly packed mass) is about 0.20 inches per second, while the rate of ignition propagation from granule to granule is around 0.30 inches per second. The speed reached in a firearm could completely ignite a charge in as little as 0.13 milliseconds. [67]

Always controversial, making black powder better has long been surrounded with rumor and superstitions (such as adding urine, wine, brandy, or straight alcohol). There definitely seems to be a positive effect of dampening the powder ingredients and letting the combination dry, beyond the obvious safety aspect of NOT grinding the dry ingredients together to achieve an integrated mix. This entire process was called *corning*, and it was begun in France as early as 1800. Modern BPs are corned and coated with graphite. Instead of forming grains by hand or with sieves, the powder was formed into a damp *mill-cake* (often with a liquid high in ammonia content such as stale urine) that was pressed in hydraulic molds to increase its density and extract the liquid. The cake was allowed to dry until it sounded like plate china when tapped. The *press-cake* was then broken into appropriate grain sizes and coated (glazed or polished) with graphite to prevent clumping. Glazing is commonly used in commercial sporting powders.

Comparison: Cap and Ball versus Modern Cartridge Weapons

Weapon System	Bullet	Pdr.	Vel.	Engy.	KD%
.31 Pocket Baby Dragoon	46gr RB	11gr	821 fps	69 ft lb	30%
.22LR Revolver	37gr LHP	FL	975 fps	78 ft lb	29%
.36 Navy Colt 1851	70gr RB	22gr	1038 fps	189 ft lb	59%
9mm ACP	88gr JHP	FL	1000 fps	189 ft lb	59%
.44 Colt New Army	141gr RB	35gr	935 fps	274 ft lb	75%
.44 Special Revolver	200gr LHP	FL	810 fps	292 ft lb	73%
.44 Colt Walker 1847	141gr RB	60gr	1287 fps	519 ft lb	87%
.41 Magnum Revolver	175gr JHP	FL	1250 fps	608 ft lb	89%

FL: Factory Load. KD%: One shot Knock Down. RB: Round Ball. HP: Hollow Point

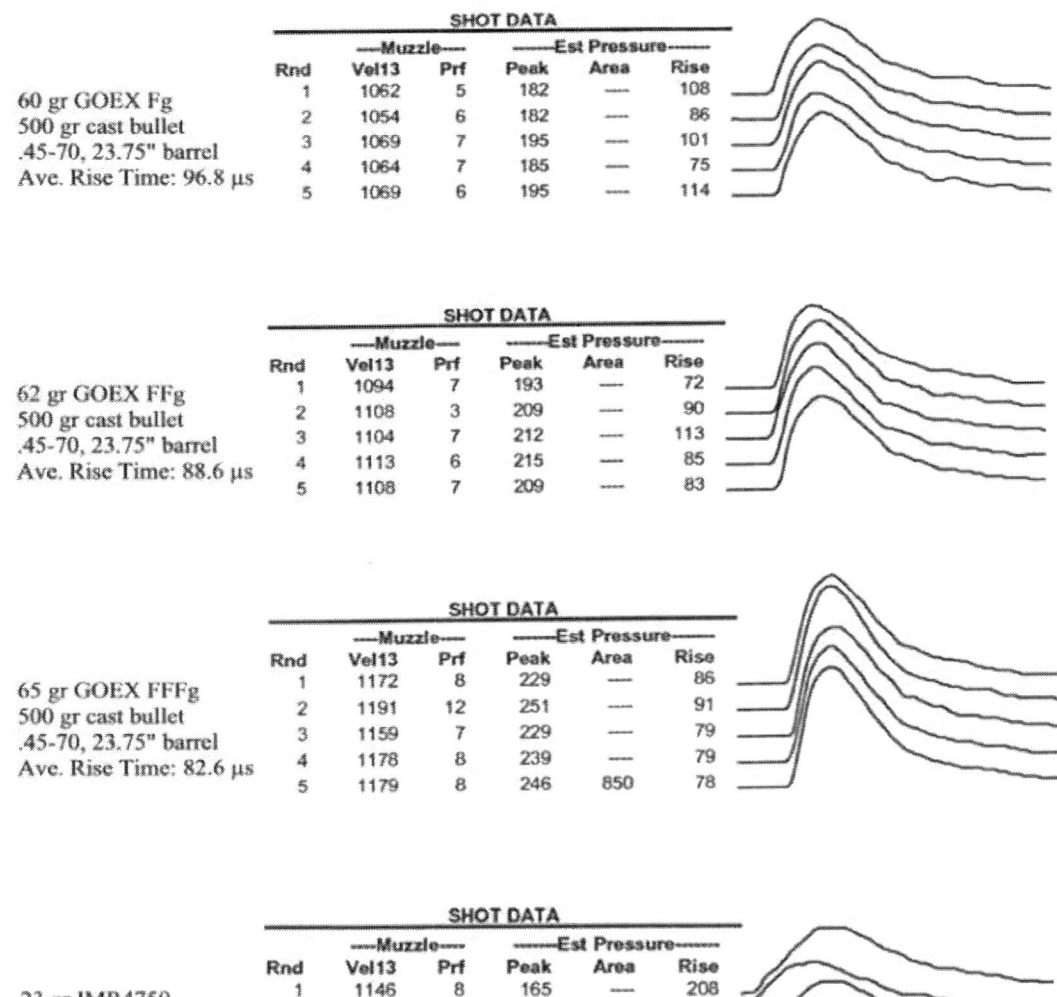

Smokeless powders are generally progressive burning powders, meaning that as the pressure increases the burn rate increases. The leading edge of the BP pressure curve will rise rapidly in a linear fashion compared to the leading edge of smokeless pressure curves, which will have more of a non-linear shape and rise slower. But smokeless powders are capable of reaching much higher pressure levels than BP—possibly four times as great. Assuming that the bullet properly seals the bore, the area under the pressure curve from the point of ignition to the time (a proxy for change in volume) the bullet exits indicates how much energy is imparted to the bullet, resulting in change in velocity. Therefore, if BP and smokeless loaded cartridges with the same bullet are fired in the same weapon and are loaded to attain the same velocity, the area under the pressure curves from the point of ignition to the time the bullet exits can be the same although the shape of the curve will be different. One thing clearly stands out - black powder, contrary to many popular assumptions, is indeed as progressive burning as smokeless powder, although smokeless has a much higher energy potential and can create higher and more sustained pressures.

The scary bit is that it is impossible to know what parts of the weapon are exposed to the higher pressures of smokeless powder before the bullet leaves the chamber or the barrel. If so, then the pressure load may be approaching the yield strength of thinner parts of the weapon and could weaken the chamber or expand the bore. Unless well versed (expert) in internal ballistics, it is best to leave the development of loading data with new powders to the experts with the proper tools, and not play around with unknown powders.[68]

About the Author

A hardened and shameless scribbler of historical nonsense, who for more than thirty years has taken his meals in front of his laptop, astride his saddle, or beside the campfire.

James M. Volo, PhD. has been teaching science and writing history for almost five decades. He is a widely published historian of daily life and military topics, and a retired physics professor with a curiosity concerning the military sciences in which he has a Masters degree. Dr. Volo was chosen to be a contributor to the 150th anniversary Essential Civil War Curriculum Project (2013). He is the author of several reference works regarding military, social, and cultural history, and has served as an historical consultant for TV and cinema productions including the PBS production *Liberty! The American Revolution* (1997), the A&E TV miniseries *The American Revolution* (1994), and the Universal Pictures movie *Sweet Liberty* (1986). An avid horseman and horse owner, he has appeared in a number of Civil War productions. He is a member of SASS and a Life member since 1972 of the NRA. He was featured in the *New York Times* (31 March 1991) for his article "Slavery in Connecticut" done for the National Endowment for the Humanities, and he hosted a segment on the C-SPAN TV series *Democracy in America, the Alex De Tocqueville* Special (1997-1998). Among his three dozen full-length published works are The Boston Tea Party, Foundations of Revolution (2012), Daily Life in Native America (2007), Blue Water Patriots: The American Revolution Afloat (2006), Daily Life in Civil War America (1998, 2010), Family Life in the 19th Century (2007), the Popular Culture of the Antebellum Period (2004), Daily Life During the American Revolution (2003), Daily Life on the Old Colonial Frontier (2002), Daily Life in the Age of Sail (2001), and the Encyclopedia of the Antebellum South (2000). Several of these are co-authored with his wife Dorothy Denneen Volo, PhD. This volume is part of the Traditional American History Series begun in 2013 that concerns the history of American liberties and American Exceptionalism. "We can only hope that other historians carry on this kind of valuable research and writing." - The Journal of Southern History

Notes and Citations

[1] R. Warshow, "Movie chronicle: The Westerner." In G. Mast, M. Cohen and L. Braudy (eds.), Film Theory and Criticism: Introductory Readings. (Oxford: Oxford University Press, 1992), 457.

[2] Fred R. Shapiro, "Who Said, 'Go West, Young Man' - Quote Detective Debunks Myths" (*CUA Magazine*, November 2007) URL: http://www.llrx.com/features/quotedetective.htm

[3] Charles Dickens, *American Notes* (1842), Kindle Location 3382.

[4] Conevery Bolton Valencius, *The Health of the Country: How American Settlers Understood Themselves and Their Land* (New York: Basic Books, 2002), 16.

[5] Alfred Thayer, Mahan, The Influence of Sea Power upon History, 1660-1783. (New York: Dover, 1987 reprint of the 1894 edition), 84-85; K. Jack Bauer, A Maritime History of the Unites States: The Role of America's Seas and Waterways. (Columbia: University of South Carolina Press, 1989), 297.

[6] See P. Lehman, Masculinity: Bodies, Movie, Culture. New York: Rutledge, 1992.

[7] Lehman.

[8] The 1975 novel by Glendon Swarthout, upon which *The Shootist* was based, was declared "one of the best western novels ever written" and "one of the 10 Greatest Western novels written in the 20th century." Western Writers of America, Spur Award Winner - "Best Western Novel" – 1975.

[9] Adams, Henry (1918). *The Education of Henry Adams: An Autobiography.* p. 417.

[10] Theodore Roosevelt, *Citizen in a Republic (a.k.a. The Man in the Arena),* a speech given at the Sorbonne, in Paris, France on 23 April 1910.

[11] J. Clinton Ransom, *The Successful Man in His Manifold Relations with Life* (New York: J. A. Hill & Co., 1889), 435.

[12] Frederick Jackson Turner, *The Significance of the Frontier in American History* (1893). URL: http://xroads.virginia.edu/~hyper/turner/

[13] Marcy 1993/1859, 24.

[14] Martha B. Caldwell, "The Stubbs." Kansas Historical Quarterly 6 (May 1937): 124-131. "The Stubbs" was a free-state militia company organized at Lawrence in April 1855 as the Kansas Rifles.

[15] Ibid.

[16] James M. McPherson: "Was It More Restrained Than You Think?" The New York Review of Books, February 14, 2008.

[17] Roderick Nash, Wilderness and the American Mind (New Haven: Yale University Press, 1971), 6.

[18] "Buffalo Hunt, 1846," Eye Witness to History (2002). URL: www.eyewitnesstohistory.com

[19] Marshall B. Davidson, "Carl Bodmer's Unspoiled West," American Heritage 14, no. 3 (April 1963): 48.

[20] David Kulczyk, *California Justice: Shootouts, Lynching and Assassinations in the Golden State.* (Word Dancer Press, 2008).

[21] Jesse Wolf Hardin, "Elfego Baca," Legends of America. URL: http://www.legendsofamerica.com/we-elfegobaca.html

[22] February 1975 issue of the *American Rifleman*.

[23] Tom Warlow, *Firearms, the law, and Forensic Ballistics* (New York: CRC Press, 2005) 105.

[24] See: Black Powder Muzzleloading Ballistics. URL: http://poconoshooting.com/blackpowderballistics.html

[25] For more technical information see The Primer Size and Bullet Diameter Chart at URL: https://www.grafs.com/uploads/technical-resource-pdf-file/12.pdf

[26] See The Firearms Guide. URL: http://www.thefirearms.guide/blog/educational/something-new-i-learned-about-the-old-38-special

[27] By Hmaag - Own work, CC BY-SA 3.0, https://commons.wikimedia.org/w/index.php?curid=12836997

[28] By Michael E. Cumpston - Own work, CC BY-SA 4.0, https://commons.wikimedia.org/w/index.php?curid=38684540

[29] S&W's production of a large N-frame revolver in .44 Magnum began in 1955; the Model 29 designation was applied in 1957. It remained primarily the province of handgun enthusiasts, some law enforcement personnel and hunters until 1971. In 1971, actor Clint Eastwood again made the .44 famous as "the most powerful handgun in the world" in the movie *Dirty Harry*. After the movie's release, retailers had trouble keeping the modern Magnum model he had used in the film in stock.

[30] Roosevelt, Theodore (2012-05-12). Hunting the Grisly and Other Sketches (p. 105). . Kindle Edition.

[31] William Wellington Greener, *The Breech Loader, and How to Use It.* (Forest and Stream Publishing Co., New York, 1892), 45.

[32] Franz Mauser, a son of the family, traveled to America in 1853 with his sister and worked at E. Remington & Sons.

[33] Similar problems had been documented against other native forces among them Zulus, Sudanese, Pashtuns, and others for the wider group of European colonial troops.

[34] Larry Schweikart, "Buffaloed: The Myth and Reality of Bison in America." URL: https://fee.org/articles/buffaloed-the-myth-and-reality-of-bison-in-america/

[35] A modern .30-30 caliber rifle round fired at such an arc will still kill a person from over 800 meters away.

[36] Earl J. Hess, The Rifled Musket in Civil War Combat, Reality and Myth (Lawrence: University Press of Kansas, 2008) 4.

[37] Sydney Vail, MD, "Stopping Power: Myth, Legend, and Reality," Police (16 January 2015). URL: http://www.policemag.com/channel/weapons/articles/2013/01/stopping-power-myths-legends-and-realities.aspx

[38] See: "The .45 Cartridge." URL: http://www.sightm1911.com/Care/45acp.htm

[39] Jim Carmichael, "Knockdown Power: Some calibers always seem to flatten game. Here's why", Outdoor Life, (31 July 2003).

[40] For further information see: Julian S. Hatcher, *Pistols and Revolvers and Their Use*, (Marshallton, Del., Small-Arms Technical Pub. Co., 1927).

[41] "Roosevelt Shot in Milwaukee," History. URL: http://www.history.com/this-day-in-history/theodore-roosevelt-shot-in-milwaukee

[42] Glen E. Fryxell, "The Lyman Devastator Hollow Point Bullets." URL: http://www.handloads.com/articles/default.asp?id=7

[43] Blaine Houmes, "The Wound of Abraham Lincoln." *Surratt Courier*, Vol. 20, No. 8, August 1995.

[44] Jan Friis-Hansen, "Mesolithic Cutting Arrows: Functional Analysis of Arrows Used in the Hunting of Large Game," *Antiquity*, No. 64, 1990, 494 – 504.

[45] Fictional spy James Bond carried each of these calibers at one time or another in his primary weapon.

[46] See URL: http://pointshooting.com/1avision.htm

[47] Jean Samuel Pauly invented an early form of centerfire ammunition, without a percussion cap, between 1808 and 1812. This was also the first fully integrated cartridge. The Frenchman Clement Pottet invented true centerfire ammunition in 1829. However, Pottet would not perfect his design until 1855.

[48] The U.S. sniper rifle in Vietnam chambered in 30-06, known for a 1,700 yard kills across open terrain, could keep an enemy battalion pinned down in favorable circumstances; but when a shooter is going to carry a couple hundred rounds through dense jungle, the smaller weight of the 223 caliber can effect what else he carries and if he will or can take more ammunition with him.

[49] In the 1960s, the 38 Special (158 grain HP semi wadcutter) was adopted as the "official" caliber of the FBI.

[50] Letter of George Washington, August 28, 1777, to Benjamin Flowers, in Washington's papers (Washington, DC: Manuscript Division, Library of Congress).

[51] On February 15, 1844, Thomas W. Gilmer was appointed U.S. Secretary of the Navy, but 10 days later he was killed with six other dignitaries by the bursting of a bow gun (a 42-pound carronade) on board USS *Princeton* while on a tour of the Potomac River below Washington, DC. Twenty other persons were injured.

[52] Nesbitt, 1994, 9.

[53] See Ole A. Haugland, "A Puzzle in Elementary Ballistics." The Physics Teacher (April 1983), 246-248.

[54] Tyson 1992, 81.

[55] See Bryant 1849.

[56] (See all: Risch, Frazer, and Miller)

[57] Robert L. O'Connell, *Of Arms and Men: A History of War, Weapons, and Aggression* (New York: Oxford UP, 1986) 191. URL: https://books.google.com/books?id=6Y8CNoQqSywC&pg=RA1-PA191&dq=Captain+Norton+Minie+1832#v=onepage&q&f=false

[58] Pat Leonard, "The Bullet That Changed History," The Opinionator (New York Times, 2012). URL: http://opinionator.blogs.nytimes.com/2012/08/31/the-bullet-that-changed-history/?_r=0

[59] See: URL: http://www.gunnersden.com/index.htm.rifle-barrel-twist-rates.html

[60] (Hess 2008, 28)

[61] Eric Hacker, "Colt Second Generation Buntline Special .45," *American Rifleman,* (November 2013, Vol. 161, Number 11: 128).

[62] Ed McGivern, *Ed McGivern's Book of Fast and Fancy Revolver Shooting*. (New York: Skyhorse Publishing Inc. 2007). 101.

[63] See Jeremy Byman, *Showdown at High Noon: Witch-hunts, Critics, and the end of the Western* (Lanham, MD: Scarecrow Press, 2004).

[64] Joyce J. Persico Newhouse, "Perfect Hero' Selleck Takes Aim at Action". *Times Union*. (18 October 1990.)

[65] The author appeared with his horse named Dasher in the film *Sweet Liberty* (1986). In a single scene, the shot was taken over and over (perhaps 20 times). At the end of each attempt, the director would yell "Back to One!" indicating that the actors needed to reset themselves for another try. Dasher quickly learned the meaning and reset himself over and over with no direction from his rider.

[66] Dabney H. Maury, Recollections of a Virginian in the Mexican, Indian, and Civil Wars (New York: 1894), 60. URL: http://docsouth.unc.edu/fpn/maury/maury.html

[67] How Fast Does Black powder Burn? URL: http://www.ctmuzzleloaders.com/ctml_experiments/bp_burning/bp_burning.html

[68] Wayne McLerren, *Black Powder Curves and Bullet Obturation*. URL: http://www.texas-mac.com/Black_Powder_Pressure_Curves_and_Bullet_Obturation.html

Made in the
USA
Monee, IL